Kerrie Dorman dived into the world of writing recently. She has had an eclectic career as well as life experiences often prone to jumping in with a motto 'Give it a go or you'll never know!' She is known in the mentoring and coaching world and lives in London with her family and occasionally her son's dog.

For my children. I love you all so, so much.

Kerrie Dorman

STAND UP

The Life Stories
of Jennie Lee

AUSTIN MACAULEY PUBLISHERS®
LONDON · CAMBRIDGE · NEW YORK · SHARJAH

Copyright © Kerrie Dorman 2025

The right of Kerrie Dorman to be identified as author of this work has been asserted by the author in accordance with sections 77 and 78 of the Copyright, Designs and Patents Act 1988.

All rights reserved. No part of this publication may be reproduced, stored in a retrieval system, or transmitted in any form or by any means, electronic, mechanical, photocopying, recording, or otherwise, without the prior permission of the publishers.

Any person who commits any unauthorised act in relation to this publication may be liable to criminal prosecution and civil claims for damages.

All of the events in this memoir are true to the best of author's memory. The views expressed in this memoir are solely those of the author.

A CIP catalogue record for this title is available from the British Library.

ISBN 9781035879694 (Paperback)
ISBN 9781035879700 (ePub e-book)

www.austinmacauley.com

First Published 2025
Austin Macauley Publishers Ltd®
1 Canada Square
Canary Wharf
London
E14 5AA

I'd like to acknowledge Premi Allen for her constant encouragement, feedback and prompts to go deeper on my emotions. Two of my dearest friends, Steph and Milly, for their memories and feedback, the others for being there. You know who you are. Victoria who holds a special place in my heart. My brother and sister for their enthusiasm to get my story out and of course my husband whose pride constantly spurs me on.

The Life Stories of Jennie Lee—The First One...

Based on the true story of a young mother's escape from domestic mental and physical abuse.

Prologue

'Stand up. For fuck's sake, STAND UP' my inner voice screamed as I cowered, completely naked on the mat inside our front door which bizarrely had 'Welcome' written on it. I barely felt the spikey bristles digging into my knees and palms although I was very, very aware that it was cold, wet and dark outside, inches away on the other side of the door. The father of my three very small children who were thankfully tucked up, fast asleep stood on the stairs in front of me about four up shouting the usual abuse, "You CuuunnnNt, you are a FAHkin cuNt, get out. Go on."

My crime? Wearing a nightie to bed.

He had ripped it off after I refused to take it off not wanting to be naked next to him in bed and the next thing that registered was being here, down on all fours on the mat. I needed to apologise quickly and a lot. Remaining where I was, I said, "I am sorry, really sorry. I won't put it on again. Please, let's just go to bed and I'll stay naked. I am sorry. Please."

I sensed a relaxation in him, all six foot two, 120 kg of him and repeated the apology. He turned and went slowly, quietly back up the stairs. Shakily, I stood up, brushed my red knees, followed him, and got back into bed where he insisted on cuddling me as there wasn't any scratchy material to irritate his skin. Finally, he dozed off; my heart rate slowed and the tears came.

To be crystal clear, I am not telling my story for pity or sympathy. Far from it. I take full responsibility for my actions and decisions. I was a strong, highly independent young woman making my way in the world. Nobody would ever have thought I would be at the receiving end of this sort of abuse. EVER. Any abuse for that matter. The point is that if **I** can be, it will be a surprise as to who in your life might be too. Abusive relationships are not just found in the home. They are everywhere. I am hoping my story will inspire at least just one person to get out, escape domestic abuse, any abuse anywhere or simply to recognise behaviour patterns and realise they are in an abusive relationship from either side. Or, to show someone you suspect might be on the receiving end, that you are there for support, you care and you deliver on that.

To note though, in my personal story, the abuser is an adult male. That is definitely not always the case, for example, *Men Do Cry* by A Dean.

Whilst this prologue is an accurate and true scenario, the rest of this book has the odd fictional slant and to protect the identity of my children, I have created Jennie Lee, who is based on me, and her children who are inspired by mine.

Chapter 1
The Unexpected Liaison

I'm Jennie Lee, mother of three gorgeous children who are at this time of writing now in their twenties. However, at the time of the prologue, they were one, two and three. Yes, a crazy breeding frenzy, because I had wonderful pregnancies and they were all very easy babies so we kept going, bang, bang, bang one after the other. Jim, Cleo and Django. I remember the first home visit by the health visitor when Django was only a week old. I happened to be in mid-nappy change with him when she and an apprentice nurse arrived. The other two were playing, running about the house and I saw a pitiful look in her eyes as if to say you poor, poor thing. I was on my own, of course, as the other half of the 'we' was busy working. Not that I minded, at all. This was my heaven. Me and my chicks.

I have auburn hair which I wear mostly in a high ponytail good ole eighties style, green eyes, freckles which are very pronounced when in the sun and a strong jaw that I often jut out when making a point or feeling defensive. There is a stud in my nose and a tattoo in a secret place. I am reasonably athletic although I know I have generous hips and 'a bottom' that fluctuates in size with my weight. I try to keep myself reasonably fit to manage this and sometimes I am on top of it and sometimes, I'm not. I have been described as sultry as well as a bit cheeky, maybe more argumentative whatever the mix, it seems I have never been short of an admirer or two.

During this period, the time of the book when they, potential admirers, see Brody, my partner and father of my children, they are scared shitless and stay well away! Which is just as well, for their sakes and as it turns out, mine. I have always been ambitious with a go-get-'em attitude bordering on precarious and often chaotic—so people describe. I've tried not to take offence to that, looking back though, I think I can see it! I have definitely been prone to diving straight in with little or zero caution—the theory being to get on with it and deal with the consequences later. I am known for speaking my mind and being completely honest; the approach to which I hope I have managed to taper over the years as my awareness levels have matured to read a situation before ploughing in! At the prologue point in my life aged 33, I had already been married and divorced, travelled extensively and studied alongside working in Sydney.

I am the eldest of three siblings close in age and bond. We had such an amazing relationship with our late mother who died from breast cancer when I was 24, my sister 22 and my brother 19. This was absolutely, excruciatingly devastating and her loss is felt every day to this very day.

The only positive outcome was the increased appreciation of our father and stepmum who had always been happy and healthy yet a new light shone as a result of our mum going. I have so much to say on this, for another story perhaps. I think looking back, it was desperately important to me to recreate that maternal relationship sooner rather than later. I have always been a capable, practical sort and for me, motherhood needed no other approach, needless to say, this (my maternal streak) was met with some surprise from my nearest and dearest as I was always partial to a party as well as hard work often burning the candle at both ends. In my early days, I was the one up on the stage, bar top or piano! The surprise factor was probably increased by who I chose to have children with. Actually, best not to sugarcoat things here, everyone was aghast, in shock, gobsmacked or whatever word makes you feel sick, thick with trepidation all of which I couldn't quite understand at the time.

This story began in the late nineties at a bar/restaurant, Oasis, in a London suburb. I was the General Manager working for a small group of shareholders. It was really hard work; however, I had a great team and it was doing well for which they rewarded me. The job came about after I had done a ski season and worked at a bar and restaurant for one of the leading ski holiday providers, the season was my solution to getting over my divorce at the grand age of 23. My first husband was kind, loving and also a bit, maybe a lot chaotic. Perhaps if I had been a little older and more experienced in life and the world, we would have made it. I was very young. Too young. Even so, whilst we were together, I experienced a great life with him. We lived in Sydney by the water and sailed on his yacht most weekends with a fun bunch of people. I was very sad that our marriage was short-lived. He was a decent guy from a respectable family. It just didn't work for me so I called it a day and went back to the UK to be with my mum and it was that winter I did the season.

Apart from all the fantastic trimmings that a ski season provides namely skiing, partying and additions to best friends, it was here working at a well-known Après Ski venue that I fell in love properly with hospitality. When I got back to London, I found the Oasis opportunity in the town where I lived, in a flat with my brother and sister which was close to our dad and stepmum.

Oasis was a small 60 covers classic wine bar and restaurant with glass floor-to-ceiling windows around half the building. In the middle was a horseshoe-shaped, solid concrete bar with rustic wooden tables and chairs that didn't completely match and big wide mirrors on the walls that weren't windows or access to the kitchen. Fun was a major factor at work. My approach was that I never asked anyone to do anything I wasn't prepared to do myself, including unblocking the loo after a busy Friday night to be ready to open Saturday morning with fully functioning facilities. Luckily, this didn't happen too often; typically, only on rugby weekends. The place had a reputation for being a bit of a pick-up joint as we strived to create a welcoming atmosphere and ladies felt comfortable coming in on their own.

Single women attract single men. There were about fifteen known engagements/marriages nurtured in Oasis. Years later, I was at a sports celebration dinner for Jim my eldest when he was sixteen and whilst standing at the bar, the lady next to me turned and said, "You're the Oasis lady."

"Yes," I said, racking my recall for her face and name. She quickly followed up with, "I met my husband in Oasis and we now have three children at this school." Warm fuzzy feeling. Some readers may remember the Ready Brek advert from the nineties where the boy who had the Ready Brek oatmeal for breakfast had a warm, red glow in his tummy for the rest of the day. **That's** the feeling. I was passionate about experiences and happy outcomes.

Anyway, on Sunday nights at Oasis, we had live music which was extremely busy. Favourite regulars came in plus we closed the kitchen and there was no food. It was one of the best nights to work for the atmosphere and I worked it most weeks.

One Sunday night, Brody walked in. I was immediately intrigued. His presence was exceedingly large. It was blatantly obvious that he was fit and strong, had a glint in his eye and was very comfortable with his own company. I felt a sense of excitement mixed with a dash of sexual apprehension. He became a Sunday evening regular and it went like this. He would come in, mainly solo after we opened at 6 pm well before the live music and order two drinks. His favourite cocktail, Campari and orange alongside a beer. The beer would disappear in a minute, he would then sip his cocktail then repeat, multiple times. He always offered me a drink and sometimes I would have one and sometimes not.

I couldn't put my finger on what I found so attractive. He had a big round head with a sharp shaved haircut. Apparently, he had been going bald a couple of years back and decided to simply shave it off. That really appealed to me, the balding-in-denial look does not! His eyes were small and brown with a neat nose. His ears had been well protected whilst being a number three rugby player which is the tight head prop one of the front row of the scrum on the right. His shoulders were massive, kept strong with daily workouts and his thighs were extremely large, solid from squats carrying enormous weights.

Apart from his size, he didn't stand out hugely to me in terms of chat or engagement. We had many, many regulars at the bar many of whom would chat us up and we each had our favourites although, at the time, I was dating a rugby player for one of the local teams who I had worked with previously. We had a good time although I didn't deem the relationship that serious, it was a bit on and off with an ex-girlfriend constantly circling. Anyhow, one evening, Brody came in and we had run out of Campari for his favourite cocktail. I was a little bit mortified. I whizzed round the corner to Tesco to pick up a bottle. He was touched by the gesture.

He said, "Ta, darlin'. You like Thai food?"

"Yes," I said.

"I'm takin' ya to eat the bes Thai food in Landern." Ah! A touch of Jason Statham there which didn't missuit the image. I noted it wasn't a question. Commanding. I liked that. Different to the normal slightly self-conscious gent I typically went for and attracted.

"Well, I'm not sure my boyfriend would appreciate that. Thanks all the same, darlin'." I said trying to mimic him whilst delivering it with a wink.

He didn't give up.

Six months later, I found myself single and eating Thai food in the best place in 'Landern' with Brody. The food was indeed absolutely delicious. The evening unearthed a few things. He was fourteen years older than me. He had been married twice previously, came with a six-year-old son and had played rugby for one of the premiership clubs although retired the year before the game went professional. Salt of the earth. His grandfather was an orphan, grew up in the orphanage Barnados. He made his mark bare-knuckle fighting before setting up his butcher and fishmonger business. He must have been a reasonably astute businessman as they earned a royal warrant of appointment. The evening was an amusing experience. He was very, very different to anyone I had been out with before which was intriguing, exciting and a little bit scary.

O myy godd...

I would use the phrase 'silent and strong' to describe Brody yet one of his characteristics that I fell for was the constant teasing glint in his eyes plus when he was in entertaining form, he was not silent. More life and soul! He made me feel feminine, protected and engaged. I remember on one of our early days out we had had a long, delicious lunch by the river and went for a stroll afterwards. We stopped at a river pub for a digestif and stood looking out over the river. He turned and looked at me and said "'ere, come 'ere, stand on this step."

Obviously, in defiance I said, "Why?"

He replied, "Don't like short birds," putting his big arms around me. This made me laugh a lot. No one had ever had this approach with me before. It was weirdly refreshing.

We laughed a lot when we were together. We had a lot of fun alone and with his friends and he spoilt me whenever I had time off with fancy restaurants as well as cooking for me at his place. Any clothes I left there, he laundered for me. Amazing, almost unbelievable. I had been wined and dined before but this experience was different. There was a new type of fizz to it.

So started the romance. It was a whirlwind. I remember lots of laughter, dinners and lunches plus Brody brought business to Oasis by way of friends and work entertaining.

Later on down the line, he and his lovely son even rolled up their sleeves to help repaint the walls.

His friends seemed to enjoy my company and I, theirs. They were an eclectic lot from all walks of life and as I am a strong believer that friends are a reliable yardstick to a person's character, this was a positive sign. There were some interesting situations though. Once, we were sitting on stools together, Brody and I at Oasis. I dropped something and slipped off my stool to bend down and retrieve it. I felt his hand on my head with a little pressure accompanied by the quip, "While ya down there…" I threw his hand off and with the other, delivered a sharp, hard slap across his face.

"I'm sorry, I'm sorry; Jesus, jus a joke," he said.

A couple of months down the track, we were in a similar situation with a friend of his. One of my favourites of his friends actually. Unbelievably, a similar thing happened. I was leaning down to get my bag and I felt his friend's hand on my head. My reaction was the same but knowing what was to follow, Brody caught my hand and said, "No, no, no, he didn mean it."

And to him, "Say ya sorry, she don' take that shi."

I received an immediate apology and what could possibly be interpreted as a nod of respect.

We moved on.

Chapter 2
Business Class and Bubbles

Before I knew it, within six weeks, he had whisked me off to Barcelona for a three-day stay. He had given me the choice of 'anywhere in the world.' Crikey. Not an offer I'd ever had before! I excitedly went about choosing where to go. It was May and I craved some serious sun, sea, and a little city excitement so I asked a regular. I always consulted the regulars; they were part of my life; Jon was a private jet pilot constantly flying to city destinations all over the world, he said Barcelona without blinking, so off we went. Business class and bubbles there and back. What a visit! There was no expense spared. We explored the city, found bars in cobbled alleyways full of old fellows and few women and ate tiger prawns on the seafront. The weather was perfect and when we reached the top of the Montjuïc Cable Car looking over the city and the hazy beyond, out of nowhere he declared that this would probably be where one day he would propose! "I'm gunna choose vis place to ask ya ta marry me, one day."

Que?

O myy godd, what the fuck? Weren't we on the fun run?

I had been very clear from the start that I was up for some fun; however, I'd be looking for my husband soon, partner and father potential to have my babies with. He made it clear that that was not on his agenda. He had done all that. So all good, all round!

Nope.

That soon changed. We fell in love. Dizzy, heady love.

After six months, he declared he definitely wanted to be that man and after twelve months, he moved in with me. Years later my family told me how they had watched on in despair. Helpless.

Anyhow, before the move, we had another trip, to Cancun, Mexico. Bring it on!

Two weeks. I lapped up the offer to be taken away again. I hadn't left Oasis for more than a week before. By this point though, I had found the amazing Victoria well, actually, she found us by literally wandering in and asking if there were any shifts going. It transpired she had been highly trained at a leading international chain and was one of the most capable people in hospitality that I had come across. Perhaps, ever. I had needed a strong number two and she was in the position to be that whilst finishing drama college, take over some key shifts of mine, which were still adding up to quite a punchy amount of hours. She became one of my best friends and a god mum—eventually. I felt safe that she was handling the cash, whilst having the ability to troubleshoot pretty much any situation plus she was fantastic, my type of fantastic with the customers. Add to that, the team, front and back of house were highly proficient and the sign of a healthy business was being able to leave it in the hands of management for a period of time. A test of buying value. The shareholders were at ease. I decided to take the leap.

I remember whilst I was grabbing a break, sitting in Oasis one afternoon post a normal buzzing lunchtime service sipping a frothy cappuccino, smoking a cigarette at my favourite round table, Brody arrived with brochures. Lots of them. It was like being a kid in a candy and toy shop all at once. He was financially covering everything. Everything. Having been the one to cover most financial things in my last two relationships, I found this act very welcome and immensely flattering. I was hooked on the fact that he was in a position to offer to do this and was choosing me to do it with. I remember precisely the minute I saw in one brochure the king-sized bed covered in rose petals and the jacuzzi bubbling away right next to it with an opened bottle of champers in an ice bucket, two glasses strategically placed in front of it.

O myy godd…why the hell not? Off we went.

Cancun is a weird as well as a wonderful place. The bed did have the rose petals on it, the sea was crystal clear and there was an intricate pool complex with cocktail bars built into the pools so the stools were in the water, only, this particular resort had been built on a swamp. O my god, the smell, the mozzies were insufferable and Brody wasn't having any of it. He cooked up the story that we were on our honeymoon which was turning into a nightmare because of the hotel circumstances. A big man, big wallet (literally old school) the resort reacted. However, the whole theme did too, we behaved as if we were on our honeymoon and chatted to other guests as newlyweds. So after the far more comfortable second week, it felt like the wedding gist had been set and I felt fine with it.

The trip was a welcome break all round as throughout this early time, Brody was going through a toxic court case with his first wife and mother of his son. She was fighting for custody to move to Australia. She had gone to the mattresses like in The Godfather! It was extremely tough for him, accused of heinous activities. He was definitely the victim.

I got on very well with his lawyer a crazy, tenacious Irishman, just as well really as he was around us a lot. He had been a longtime loyal friend of Brody's, who explained very quietly to me that it was touch and go and my support along with a bit of distraction was welcome. The insinuation that I could help made me happy and needed.

The situation sickened me actually.

Having come from divorced parents myself, I knew neither one of them would have considered any move without the other along with the repercussions of any lack of access either one would have to us three. Their divorce was so amicable that lunches together with step-parents happened at handovers. This angle of attack from Brody's ex wife was alien and horrific to me, made worse as I was building my own relationship with Brody's son.

I understood the ex-wife's need for a fresh start yet this six-year-old boy would probably see his father once maybe twice a year. There is no way a relationship would continue and grow as a parent-child should; I felt very strongly that she had piled the entire responsibility and blame for the status quo of their relationship outcome onto him to fuel her case. Well, we all know that blame is never fully that of one person although it is very easy to exonerate ourselves or another if it's convenient. And most of the time it is. Convenient. Taking on and accepting blame for a situation is extremely difficult as well as uncomfortable.

Anyway, the final outcome was a good one and Brody's son stayed in England and became very much part of our lives, with us every other weekend and they spent Tuesday afternoons together. This close, upfront insight into fatherhood as an adult, was fascinating to me and the fight of a dad to keep his son in his life was inspiring. Their relationship was happy and he **seemed** a great father. He was always on time to pick him up, made sure he did his homework and spent time asking about his week and what was happening at school. They laughed a lot together.

As I was no stranger to step relationships, I took my responsibility seriously trying to make sure that whilst he was with us they had enough dad/son time together, not stepping on his mum's toes and having as much fun as possible. He was a really great kid, especially considering everything that was going on around him. I knew he had an inkling as to what that was but he remained loyal to both his parents. I enjoyed his time with us and looked forward to his weekends.

I do remember though on reflection that I was probably quite annoying on the parenting front. At the time all I knew about parenting was my own upbringing, which had had a very different approach, and initially, I would comment on a regular basis on things such as…'More than one ice cream a day was excessive and spoilt'—Brody would give him up to three or four.

'He is old enough to cut up his own food'—Brody always offered to cut up his meat. After a while, Brody called me out on this approach, "FaHkin shu'up. You don' have any kids, I do!" Slightly harsh; nevertheless, it was the Brody way which was becoming the norm for me. Point taken just the same. A first lesson.

Everyone has their own way and I have since learnt from experience that when you become a parent, it is very much your prerogative to parent how you see fit which is hopefully influenced by what you have taken, positive and negative from exposure to any other parenting. We all have our individual approach and it is a grand ole learning curve with many to judge you.

So here I was, an official partner, stepmother, and international jet setter in roughly twelve months. Oh how things can change! It felt wonderful, an instant little family, a mini box on my maternal agenda was ticked; Brody and I were on the same life page wanting to be together forever and I loved my job, passionately.

Chapter 3
The Local Jungle Drums

Meanwhile, during all this time the local town jungle drums were rumbling.

As with any small town, everyone knew everyone; especially when it came to the rugby community. We as a family were loyal, invested and extremely active supporters of the local club. It came as no surprise to me that according to this network, Brody's reputation was somewhat dodgy/shifty. One member of the rugby community, I think he was a local coach and a peer of Brody's said to my father, "I wouldn't be allowing my daughter anywhere near him," to which my dad jokingly pointed out that I was 28 and his daughter was six, correctly implying I was of my own (fiercely) strong mind but he was quick to relay the conversation to me. Again I thought it was just a hilarious retort as opposed to the message it carried and so the rhetoric continued on my deaf ears.

My 28th birthday celebrations, more or less a month after Barcelona included a BBQ at my parents with a handful of my closest, oldest girlfriends, some of whom hadn't met him yet. Brody and his best mate who was and still is a respected member of the international rugby community, my parents, of course, and a friend or two of theirs. We had been together about twelve weeks at this point.

I arrived early to help with food, the table and hosting stuff. When I got into the house, there was an extremely impressive bunch of two dozen red roses. Absolutely beautiful. I remember being very touched and excited by them. My dad clocked the excitement and said, "You know, I used to send young ladies flowers like that precisely to get your sort of reaction."

Well, instead of registering what his message actually was, I saw my dad in a new light as to what he was like as a young single man. I'd never guessed that he would have been the romantic sort.

O myy godd...

What he really wanted to get through to me was how easy it was to impress and undress. After the BBQ, one of my most forthright, upfront friends gave me the overall general feedback which was, "What the fuck are you doing with this guy?"

Roughly around the same time my two besties from skiing asked me to bring Brody round for supper. They weren't at the birthday BBQ for some reason and were yet to meet him. I arrived first straight from Oasis with a chilled bottle of wine. We were chatting away when he arrived. It was just the four of us and I felt we were in a safe environment.

Dinga ling – why did I need to feel that?

Anyway, a little later than he was expected he arrived all suited and booted with his leather briefcase.

'Oh hi its so good to meet you Brody we have heard so much about you come on in.' Said one of the besties.

'You look smart.' I said.

'Thanks darlin' yeh. well, fought' I'd make the effuurt for court.' I knew he'd been at court all day in the ongoing custody battle which I hadn't really delved into with anyone. It was his news not mine.

'Ah,' said the other bestie, a lawyer. 'Does your work include legal cases?' and before I could say anything...

'No luv, I'm bein' taken ta court for abusin' my son.'

Okayyyyyyyyyyyy.

The dynamic and atmosphere in the room changed dramatically. They weren't sure if asking further was ok, I hadn't prepared them, and he fell silent lapping up the shock. However, he was just telling the truth, and I was in love. I excused his idiosyncrasies on the pretence that he was just getting to know everyone rather than the cold hard fact that he was simply a rude fucker.

My uncle, a calm man with a gentle manner of whom I am very fond, said to me early on after the first whispers of a marriage...

"Jennie, if I was a 41-year-old man I would want to marry you too..." I simply took this as a massive compliment rather than the warning that it was and replied, "Thanks soo much, Uncle Albie, that's really sweet."

O myy godd again! Now, looking back and from a helicopter view, re-running that situation in my mind, I can feel and see my parents who were present, their disbelief oozing out of every orifice.

But, what would I have said if they sat me down that very moment and said, "No, Jennie, you're not getting it."

I can take an educated guess that I would have been offended and very probably held the conversation against **them**. You see when someone is in this frame of mind, as was I, you have to let them live it out. More so for people with a strong will like me. There is little point in alienation unless there is a safety issue and at this point, there wasn't. Interestingly though, just before this occasion, I had had my eyebrows shaped by waxing. A small bruise was left just above my right eye. As soon as my father spotted it, he asked in a very concerned manner how I got the bruise. In hindsight, it was obviously on their minds that Brody was capable of being physical with me and I interpreted that correctly at the time. But they didn't know him as I knew him. He would never do that.

Around the same time that summer, there was a charity event at the local rugby club. The town was out in force. It was a sunny day the Pimm's and beer were flowing. We arrived separately and I tracked down my parents to say hi and then ventured to find Brody. I found him in a deck chair with his shirt off next to an equally large man also with his shirt off. He was an ex-rugby player from Brody's club, also front row. They had pints in their hands. I went straight up and gave him a kiss.

"Blimey ooze vis then?" The other chap said.

I introduced myself. He looked at Brody and said, "Ah. You gotta posh bird."

I winked and said I was off to get a drink. Brody laughed his big belly laugh and I giggled to myself. I liked being a 'posh bird.' At the same event, I bumped into a regular from our favourite rugby pub where we often went for a drink pre-games, when I wasn't working. I hadn't seen her in a while and she asked how things were.

"Oh," I gushed. "I'm madly in love!"

"That's fantastic," she said, "who with?"

"Brody Brown."

She looked at me long and hard; her smile slowly dried up. She must have been jealous.

Back at Oasis, the shareholders were aware of my new love interest. One of them came in regularly on a Monday to have lunch with friends, whoever was around. I was able to join them on occasions. When I was invited on one particular Monday around this time, I was sitting at the favourite lunch club table with them when Brody came in.

"Ah!" I said, "Finally, I can introduce you to Brody." And to him, "Join us." He had about a half hour before meeting a client and so he did.

The conversation that followed seemed to me to be fairly pleasant so I was extremely confused when he left to greet his client, the shareholder turned to me and said with a mild look of shock, "This is the new **boyfriend**, Brody?" I confirmed this was true to which he said to me...

"You are joking. What exactly is it that is sparking your interest?"

Oh myy godd, him too.

What was wrong with everyone? Was it the accent? Not quite home county? Well, actually it was so far from it; it just wasn't worth making the comparison or asking that question. People just needed to get to know him, why were they judging immediately?

"Lots of things actually." I replied mumbling a thanks for lunch and leaving the table as soon as was polite. The next time, I joined the Monday lunch club, the topic of Brody did not arise. It never did after that. Occasionally, they were in at the same time and Brody would nod pleasantly and offer to buy him a drink. This was always refused though, but with a thank you.

Life continued. I simply started avoiding the negative people.

Chapter 4
Family Wrangles

An important conversation Brody and I had that I should share was, whilst we were eating prawns and drinking rose in the sun by the sea in Barcelona and please remember this was very early on, six weeks in, was of the bond and love I have for my brother and sister. My mother had passed away just two years previously at this point and we were closer than ever. I could tell he couldn't quite understand it when I said they came before anything/anyone else.

The dynamics of his own family were coming out bit by bit. When I write the word 'dysfunctional' I mean it was so conflicting, alien like to me as I had never come across anything quite like it in my whole life and I found it very sad.

They were riddled with unrest, money being the cause, breeding greed with zero ability to communicate which led to all sorts of issues as you can probably imagine.

His grandfather, the orphan, who had grown into an ambitious young man, had become a bare-knuckle fighter. Married a farmer's daughter. Initially, it was a happy marriage and they had three children, two girls and a boy. Brody was the son of the youngest daughter who fell pregnant with

Brody's elder brother in wedlock at the age of seventeen, shortly followed by Brody.

Brody was very close to his uncle, who was incredibly supportive of him, watching his rugby matches and lending him his Roller (Rolls Royce) to impress the ladies. He worked for his father in the butcher and fishmonger business in Kensington which had gained its royal warrant by this point and as soon as he could, Brody joined them. I think he was sixteen or seventeen by which point his mother had moved him to his grandmother's to live as parenting was a bit tough for her. Poor thing. This meant that Brody and his grandmother became extremely close. She did everything for him, including warming his underpants at five in the morning before going to work at the butcher. That was quite sweet.

Anyway…by this point, the grandfather had left her for a younger newer version and she never quite got over the heartache. When he died, there was a family feud over the money. It all went to the newer younger version except the actual shop which went to Brody's uncle until Brody was to turn 21 at which point half of the business should have gone to Brody. When the time came, his uncle refused. Naturally, Brody fought for his rightful half.

There was a highly disruptive family controversy. His grandmother sided with her son, not grandson. She ceased seeing and speaking to Brody as did the uncle. His mother didn't really care. This unexplained turn of the state of relationships I believe had a deep, lasting, highly detrimental effect on him. These days, one might seek some help and support in the form of coaching or counselling to deal with anger and betrayal. Shortly after this, his parents who ran kennels from their land lost their licence because his mother had dropped off a dog in the middle of one of the major airports due to an overdue invoice. I struggled considerably with this whole situation. Poor innocent dog. It would have been so frightened not to mention that anything could have happened to it. Luckily, it was scooped up by the authorities and did eventually get returned to its owner.

Brody and his brother were able to take over the licence on behalf of their parents so that they could keep their business. The parents breached all the improvement requirements and blamed the brothers, their sons who, not only faced extortionate fines were then left to sort out the multiple issues themselves. Ten years of not speaking followed.

This whole dire state of relationships had recently thawed and appeared on the mend as I was coming onto the scene. Interessstinggg.

One summer, we went to find his grandfather's grave which was on one of the Balearic islands where we were holidaying. We found that between all three of his children, Brody's mother included, no one had paid for his gravestone as was required. To be clear they were all wealthy, completely able and in the position to afford to do so, so it had just been removed, probably replaced by another. They didn't care. This made me extremely sad. I could tell it affected Brody too.

'FaHkin' CunTs.' He said.

Despite all this background, at the time I was introduced to the family, as I mentioned the emotional ice was thawing and they seemed to be in a reasonable space. Although, when Brody took me up to meet them and stay a night, we arrived at about 7.30 pm, his mum was in bed watching TV. His dad was reading with a cup of tea and most of the lights in the house were out. A bit weird? Maybe if they were old but they were just 60. Well, she was. He was a couple of years older.

Anyway, despite my initial gnawing of the gut I focussed on the fact that at least they had come together to support Brody in his fight to keep his son and I had to keep remembering that. Plus each to their own. I just knew that I'd be doing things very differently when it was eventually my turn. Maybe they were simply just tired of his wives and partners by the time I came along His mother was taking the stand as some sort of witness for him in the custody case. I can't remember the details though. In our first year, we saw them from time to time, reasonably often and at Christmas, I got a present. What was lovely was that the cousins were so close, the three boys. Brody's son and his two nephews. Then! One Sunday, they all met at Oasis; we joined them for lunch. It seemed like a happy affair. Family chit-chat and the boys cracking jokes and being silly. They certainly liked the food which was ordered in abundance. The bill came and I took off 30% which was above the normal staff 25% discount. I think I wanted to show them goodwill, be welcoming and probably appreciation for the custom too. Well, that was it for me. I was persona non grata from that moment on. Cut out. I couldn't understand it.

The discount wasn't big enough, Brody explained a couple of months later. They were expecting the meal, the whole meal for free, I think. I was never quite sure. I have seen them twice in total, to this date, after that.

Then came the saddest of all. His parents groomed, as in lured their eldest grandchild, Brody's nephew to leave his parents and live with them to help run the kennels and farm.

They promised him all their wealth, including the big house, kennels and land. He had scarcely turned 14 years old and not knowing how to handle the situation, simply ceased contact with his parents. God only knows what he was being told, persuaded or more to the point, brainwashed to fill their own needs. Needless to say, Brody's brother and his wife were absolutely devastated. It nearly broke his mum. His dad had a stroke a few years later and was never quite the same.

"Don't ever let them get close if you have kids," she said to me. There was categorically, no chance of that I thought.

The common detest that Brody and I had for his parents over this last act brought us even closer together. We discussed preventing his son and any future children we had from seeing them. I was relieved and he was calm, unsurprised even. I found it an extremely strange and mournful situation. Both sets of my grandparents had been involved with us as kids and whilst there were different types of relationships on either side, I had loved them very much. Grandparents bring a different type of love. Wiser, distanced, outside but inside views; so very important to contribute to a well-rounded childhood.

So I guess the concept of a close bond within a family did not resonate with him, was completely foreign and meant absolutely nothing. Maybe he digested it as a challenge to infiltrate mine and break the bond; either way, his story was prophetic of future convictions and it should have been a very loud ring-a-ding-ding for me.

My sister was living in Sydney at this time. I remember telling her I had met this terrific man albeit a wee bit older, I was having a really good time. My brother was working locally in his first job post uni and as well as living together, he would pop in all the time for coffee, post-work drinks and dinner which was really cool. Even so, the time came when he wanted a stint in Sydney too, a move I encouraged. Breathing Aussie air for a bit, especially when you have citizenship is a no-brainer. This led to discussions about Brody moving into the flat with me once my brother had flown off and to the disbelief of everyone around me, this is what happened.

In he moved, with all his stuff! *There was soo much.* He was a hoarder. Slowly, it all found homes in nooks and crannies. The flat was actually a duplex. The top two floors of a Georgian semi; roomy, light, airy and carpeted throughout. It had stairs leading from the front door up to a landing which had one bedroom, shower and loo and a door into a spacious open-plan kitchen, dining and sitting room with big windows at either end, a bay at the sitting room side which looked out onto the tops of the trees lining the road below. Nestled in the bay was my mum's baby grand piano. I had tried so hard to keep this with me wherever I went. It was special and I honestly thought that one day, I would actually get round to playing again. Well, my play repertoire at the time of writing remains chop sticks and the start of Boogie-Woogie. There is still time! On top of the piano were numerous picture frames of special people and a lot of us three siblings.

Up the next flight of stairs halfway was another big window with a border of blue and red stained glass. I loved this window. It was pretty and it lit up the whole landing on both levels. At the top was a decent-sized bathroom again with a large window, two double bedrooms and what really could only ever be a study. It did actually become Brody's study. In went his desk, big chair and paperwork. His client files were thick with documents probably helped by the fact that each sheet was photocopied three times. I never got to the bottom of exactly why, I'm not even sure one copy went with the client! Hey ho.

Even though the flat felt 'full' this seemed like a very natural next step, his stuff with my stuff, his son coming every other weekend and they had their afternoons together. We fell into a routine.

And then the jewellery purchases started. It was all a bit hazy as to how exactly. I think when we had the conversation about him moving in, the realisation that the fun year had taken course to a serious long-term outlook, including children; he wanted to buy me a ring to solidify it all. Plus we had had the Cancun holiday where we had pretended to be newlyweds on honeymoon and he had started referring to me often as 'the wife.' Anyhow, it kicked off all unofficially as in not an official engagement ring, we called it our love ring. It was impressive. His friends were full of praise and happiness. Mine were full of scepticism. My family in shock. They simply didn't get him yet.

"He is not very…endearing," My father said to me clearly struggling to find a word to portray his point without offending me. He had taken me out for a pub lunch when the 'love ring' had been noticed. I brushed this aside with a reply on finding the strong, silent type attractive.

My lovely sister came back for a visit and of course, stayed with us in the flat. It was still a third hers! I was excited for her to meet Brody although quietly apprehensive and as it eventually turned out, with reason. Needless to say, she is **not** a Jason Statham fan. It did not go well. On the run-up to her arrival, I had been soo looking forward to seeing her. We are exceptionally close and it had been over a year since we'd seen each other. I got her room all ready and planned a few things we could do together. Unbeknown to me, this ignited a highly detrimental, deep rooted reaction as Brody felt completely threatened. Maybe he remembered the conversation in Barcelona or maybe it was literally that he had to share my attentions. But he had been fine, the opposite, with my brother, maybe because he had been there from the very beginning. Who knows. I can only thread it back to when she called one day from Sydney, pre-visit and he answered the phone.

"Ello?"

She probably said something like, "Hi, its Jennie's sister…"

"Alright, darlin, how ar ya?"

Silence. She may have been slightly shocked at the way he spoke which I believe he took as entitled judgement.

After a couple of seconds and no further chat, he shouted, "Out to me Lee, ya blister's on the dog."

I'll translate for those who are not familiar with cockney rhyming slang.

Blister comes from skin and blister = sister.

Dog and bone is a phone, so literally it means 'Ya sister's on the phone.'

She asked me who that had been and my answer was also followed by a long silence.

So, it was the first time they had met. He was off hand, rude, disinterested and tried on some shock tactics; for example, announcing he sat down to take a pee, whilst we were in the middle of an unrelated conversation and completely ignoring her when entering a room.…All to gauge her reaction. I ignored all this as getting a reaction from me was equally a priority. I felt her total dismay. But she would never understand the reasons behind it all and I felt protective over him. We didn't discuss it. I think neither of us wanted any confrontation, we just weren't wired that way. She returned to Sydney. It felt awful.

Soon after she went back, I met Lady Fiona. It must have been whilst networking locally because I remember her giving me her business card or 'calling card' as she put it. Lady Fiona gave etiquette sessions. O myy godd…just what Brody needed. Would he go for it? I explained my situation and relationship and she gave me an overview of what a session might achieve. I put it to him, it would be a joint visit, something to do together, good for networking. Surprisingly, he was quite up for it.

We sat on her sofa looking smart. We had dressed up a little and drank tea out of teacups with saucers and teaspoons. During the session, she went over the importance of manners and how we have the power to make someone feel relaxed, comfortable and at ease. Well, you would have thought **he** was the expert! He had all the chat and charmed Lady Fiona who, at the end of the session, gave me a quizzical look as if to say, in the best manner possible of course, 'What the fuck are you talking about?'

So, he was absolutely choosing to be rude. Why weren't any alarm bells ringing? I felt deflated and relieved all at the same time. It was in there, I just needed to do more to draw it out. I was a little baffled not to mention quite hurt though as to why he wouldn't do this for me anyway. Not being rude. Simply not his true self, I guess.

It was around this time that he gave me the 'united front' chat. I think he sensed that I was feeling there were cracks appearing in the romance. Maybe, he genuinely thought the same and wanted to get back on track. We were out for pizza one night and he said, "Listen…we have a good fing 'ere. I larve ya so very very much and I know ya larve me so very very much bu' we need to 'ave a uni'ed fron' ta move forward and make vis really work."

Well, that struck something inside of me. I wanted a united front. I wanted to be the person who provided him with solid love and a stable family environment. What I didn't ask was, what that looked like exactly, for him.

In retrospect, I should have asked him to describe it so we understood each other's definition of a united front. Nonetheless, I didn't ask that, I agreed and on we went.

Next came a beautiful necklace. It was called Tiger Heads. I loved it. People wanted to touch it. It was magnetic and it made me feel even more so that I belonged to him. We belonged together.

With both my brother and sister in Sydney and Brody ensconced in the flat, chat started around buying them out. This happened. I can only imagine the sort of conversations the family were having about it. They have since alluded that it was an extremely tough time for them. He was around for the long haul. They just could not get it. Confusion as to my mental state was on many agendas, apparently.

Life carried on and we were facing the year 2000. Big global uncertainty over computer software being able to cope with the number 2000 as a date. Would all data be erased? No one knew. I wasn't too concerned; I was more occupied with making the decision of holding a big fuck off event at Oasis to see in the new century or trying to rent it out. Customers didn't know what they were doing, although the underlying theme it seemed were parties at home. The licensing laws were a bit stringent for such an event. We ended up renting it to a trusted regular of whom I was very fond and I just handed over the keys. Brody and I ended up there on the way home from where we had been, a big house party at a great friend of **his.** I loved this friend.

She was bright, bubbly and soo much fun so I didn't question that we had not been invited to join any of **my** friends. Coincidentally, her father knew mine reasonably well through rugby although the link didn't seem to reassure my dad at all. Anyway, it was a great night. We danced, ate and drank there and then more at Oasis. Needless to say, the computers were all fine. The world sighed in relief.

The year held much in store for me. Oasis was going to have a big makeover and refurbishment. I was whisked off for Lunch in Luxembourg for my 29th birthday and Brody was taking me back for a visit to Sydney. And I was going to fall pregnant.

Chapter 5
Falling Pregnant

I fell pregnant with Jim on the trip to Sydney, via Florida. The travel team was Brody, his son and I. Our first trip all together. We were all extremely excited. Brody was always in a good mood on our trips because he had my undivided attention plus, we were doing things he wanted to do and be with people he wanted to be with. Happy days. The lead-up to leaving had been on the crazy side preparing the plans for Oasis to have its refurb whilst we were away. It was a fairly major project and it was going to substantially upgrade the place and increase capacity by twenty covers. I had been given carte blanche to design, budget and engage with builders obviously, the ultimate sign-off was down to the shareholders although they knew that I knew the business inside out and what it needed for its next growth spurt.

The planned closure was for six weeks which was an opportune time to take an extended holiday during the middle three. The builders and architect were local, reliable friends and there was nothing I could do for the majority of the time that the core work was going on. Plus, I had Victoria who had taken a break prior to our holiday, to keep tabs on progress and we'd be in close contact.

We had one situation to dampen our or rather my excitement. One of my fab team who had personally just been through an extremely tough time was living in the flat upstairs above the restaurant. The work was making it impossible for her to stay there so I offered her our flat whilst we were away. We were using it to store the bar stools and a few things that wouldn't fit in the stock room but there was lots of room, and I liked the idea of her being there. I knew she would treat it with respect plus I felt so much for her. She was such a lovely young lady; she had recently lost her mum yet been treated appallingly by her previous employer. A woman. I have since stopped assuming that fellow women automatically look out for other women. In fact, there's a whole other story here too! Anyway, when I explained the plan to Brody, he exploded.

"There's no faHkin way she is stayin' 'ere. JESUS, she's seeing that Schwartz an I'm not 'avin him in 'ere nikin' my stuff."

Schwartz is a last name of German/Yiddish (German-Jewish) origin, meaning 'black'. Her boyfriend was black.

Ohhhh, myyyy godddd.

She burst into tears when I explained I'd made a mistake. Not surprisingly. She had nowhere else to go. I felt horrific and ashamed of myself. It was pathetic. Very sadly this was becoming usual, the fact that I hadn't fought back. Stood up to him. I could have to come to a reasonable, honest arrangement with her as in perhaps, no guests?

Should I have? Of course, I should have. Big and bold my usual style. And worst case, fuck the trip. Absolutely nothing can excuse this behaviour. But, all I could see and feel was that I had to stand by him plus, he now owned half the flat.

Sooo off we went. On the day of departure, I happened to be on my period and completely forgot to take any birth control pills. I honestly had the naive idea that because I'd been on the contraceptive pill for nearly fourteen years, it would all be ok in terms of falling pregnant. This was confirmed by Brody as clearly his experience of the female cycle was highly accomplished.

Looking back, I know that if I was truly worried about falling pregnant; there were other options, for example, using a condom! Brody was unworried and thought we should crack on with a kid anyway. He wasn't getting any younger! At this point, he is 43.

We three embarked on one of the most fantastic of trips, courtesy of Brody, of course. One of his best girlfriends owned a successful hotel in the golfing district of Florida. The other best girlfriend who introduced them was meeting us there with her husband (A Scottish international rugby player—a future god dad) and their one-year-old son. It was soo much fun. We were completely spoilt. Together, we laughed, ate, drank, explored, went horse riding and alligator spotting and had two nights at Disneyland. Brody's son and I became even closer simply due to being together every day, living together albeit holiday living, sharing new experiences and we left feeling on top of the world and very happy. Whilst in Florida, my period finished.

The Sydney section of the trip had a slightly different tone. I was of course apprehensive as the last time I had seen my sister was in London when she had first met Brody. My brother and she were sharing a house with a friend of his from uni who I knew well and whilst I knew clearly where she stood on the Brody front, I was hoping that he was still positive despite what I knew my sister would have reported back from her trip.

However, my sister was amazing. She totally rose above the London experience and made our trip the best it could be. She organised drinks with old friends, dinners together and trips for me to show the place to Brody and his son. When thinking about where to stay, it seemed obvious to book my mum's old favourite, The York Apartments. It was in central Sydney and familiar. When we were shown our apartment, I took a breath as it was the exact same one that Mum and the family had stayed in for my wedding. I woke up in this apartment on the wedding day of my failed marriage. Now if you are spiritually minded, you may take this as a sign. Or it could just be that only some of the apartments in the block are available for short lets and not so much of a coincidence. I look back and want to feel the spirits sending a warning message. Obviously, the spirit of my mum. Although it did not, it purely made me feel she was around. No warning. However, after a long Sunday lunch with the three of them, my brother, sister and friend at the tail end of the trip, my brother said, "Come for a drink, Jen."

Brody was taking his son back for a shower and bed. I could feel his hackles rise. He wanted me to come back with him of course. I looked at him. For the first time, I felt irritated. I remember hoping it wasn't visible. There weren't any repercussions so I guess not, but I really was. I wouldn't be seeing my brother for another year or so. Why would he not want me to spend as much time as possible with him? Now I know, that it was because he was insecure. His subconscious would have been sending a message that not being there meant he couldn't control the situation; we might talk about him and more so was the injustice of me being out having one more drink whilst he was on father duties.

I said gently, with a calm voice, "I'll just have a quick drink whilst you do bedtime stuff and I'll meet you back at the flat. You'll barely notice that I'm not with you."

We went to a bar on the way back to our apartment block so I was going in the right direction. It was just my brother and his friend. My sister had left earlier. We bought drinks, nestled into a booth and then it came. The chat.

"So Jen, what's the long-term plan with Brody?" I explained that there were kids planned and that one day we'd move to a house. They took the age slant. Did I not think that he was too old? By the time a baby came around, he'd be mid-forties and mid-fifties when the child was ten. It took energy to be a hands-on active father. This approach didn't bother me. Brody was extremely fit and addicted to exercise with no sign of letting up anytime soon. I took the feedback with grace and got back to the apartment before my absence started antagonising Brody. Nonetheless, it was a truly wonderful holiday and so great to spend time with my siblings and friends from before.

On our return, I was keen to check on progress at Oasis. We had two weeks to go to reopening day. It was not good. Whilst I had been away, the head builder had also been away and left his brother in charge. They were so behind. The morning I was there, the building team rolled in at 9.20 am. No bloody wonder! We went through the schedule of work and timeframe. It was clearly going to be touch and go. Thankfully, the head builder was back the next day and we moved into supercharge mode, all hands on deck!

Victoria and I became site lackeys, clearing, moving, and then helping to paint. The night we reopened was a classic hospitality scene. Mayhem behind closed doors with calm smiling faces to customers front of house! The kitchen team now operating in a smaller space had managed to cook up samples of bar snacks and starters to hand around which went down soo well. It felt great. Around 10 pm, I sat down to have a glass of wine. It tasted very strange. I checked the bottle which also smelt strange, so did the next glass and the next. Victoria said they were all fine. I must be sick or at least coming down with something. Maybe the fight against time to re-open had taken its toll.

The next week was extremely busy with oodles of renewed interest from regulars in the refurbishment as well as the refreshed wine list and menu. We were buzzing. The shareholders were happy. It was at the end of this week that a few things dawned on me. We had left for Florida over five weeks ago. My period was late. My wine intake had been vastly reduced due to appetite, not time.

Ohh myy godd. Pregnant?

I had not been physically sick or anything else, for example, feeling nauseous. The only clue was the smell and taste of wine. I bought a pregnancy test and took it home to do together with Brody the next morning. I think it had to be the first wee of the day back then, for an accurate result. Sooo there we were, together in the bathroom even before a cuppa and did the test. Sure enough, there followed two bright pink lines. Positive. I was pregnant! We looked at each other and I started giggling. He smiled. Right, what the fuck now? I guess book an appointment with our doctor. I loved our doctor, not that I was there very often, but he was just very cool as he continued to be when we both rocked up for our appointment a few days later. He took more tests as well as the usual on heart rate and blood pressure which were all very healthy.

He confirmed I was indeed pregnant and explained what was to happen next, the process and the hospital choices. I was sooooo excited. Brody and I agreed that we would keep quiet until the three-month scan which took forever to come around. Meanwhile, I felt pretty good. A little exhausted at times. Maybe one morning, a vague sense of nausea but I think that had more to do with an over-brewed cup of tea. I still get that a bit now. What I did feel about a hundred times a day was that Ready Brek warm fuzzy feeling every time I remembered I had a tiny, little person growing inside of me. I refer to it now as cooking them, my babies, until they were ready to come out and face the world. Not one of them came early or on time. They were all nearly two weeks late. Just too comfy being cooked.

Finally, the scan came around. We drove together to the hospital. Brody appeared excited too, well, for him anyway! Then before I knew it, I was on the couch, belly covered in gel and the outline of Jim's minuscule body came up on the screen whilst the nurse checked for all fingers, toes, eyes and ears and did the neural scan. He was all there! I didn't know the baby was Jim as we didn't discover the gender until he popped out, the knowledge is in retrospect.

This was the most amazing thing in the whole wide world. Then we heard his heartbeat. Well, I was in tears and Brody was holding my hand tightly, smiling. Wow.

I was soo excited I called my nana in Sydney and told her the news immediately. I described the scene we had just come from, somewhat beside myself and she could hear it in my voice. She was very happy for us she said.

Next, it was Dad to whom to break the news. He popped into Oasis to see me as requested over the next few days. I took him to the quiet side of the bar and told him. He looked at me, "Is that good?" He said, clearly not knowing whether to show happiness or concern.

"Yes! Yes!" I said. I was eager for him to be happy for me.

"Well, then that's great. How are you feeling?"

I explained I was feeling healthy, tired on occasion yet generally very well and very excited. I asked him if he would pass on the news to my stepmum which he promised to do. I didn't hear from her for three days. When I called her, I was worried that Dad hadn't let her know, but he had. She just didn't know what to say. I put it down to her being very busy. She was still working full-time in a high-powered demanding role. More to the point, probably mournful.

So life went on. I released the news to the shareholders, Victoria and the team, customers, and friends. Reactions to my face were overall, cautious yet congratulatory. God only knows what they were after I left the room.

I completely and utterly loved being pregnant. It was a wonderful experience for me. I know some suffer. I counted myself lucky. I had always been fascinated by pregnancy. How our bodies could make and grow another. I didn't miss the alcohol or the smoking.

That's not to say I didn't have the odd glass of wine with my evening meal. In fact, when we went out to eat Brody always ordered a nice bottle of red and I would have a glass. Towards the end of my pregnancy bubbles helped with digestion so the odd cold beer was my treat. I definitely didn't miss the smoking. Yuk. It smelt disgusting. Funny how your body creates natural reactions like that. The exhaustion stage flourished into the blooming stage, and I started putting on the real weight. The chef at Oasis didn't help. He kept saying, "Come on, you are eating for two now!"

"But one of us has a tummy the size of a Pinhead." I would reply.

Nevertheless, he made me all my favourite dishes which I just could not refuse. If ever there was a time to eat all your favourite dishes all the time, wasn't it when you were pregnant? Delicious and such a treat at the time, but not so appreciated when you're trying to shift it after the baby arrives. I ended up gaining four stone.

O myy godd.

What a shock when Jim came out and three and a half stone stayed put! I had to keep wearing my maternity clothes. I did learn from this though.

I remember his first kick. I was at home on the sofa after a busy day and Brody was cooking us some dinner. I felt this flutter inside. Like butterflies. I called Brody but he missed it.

"Don't worry, darlin', it'll 'appen all ve time now," he said, the expert!

I got busy preparing the baby's room. It was my sister's old room which I repainted a bright yellow. I kept her double bed in there with the cot. It was cozy which felt right plus I had an inkling that I would be sleeping in there a bit with the baby in the first month.

My new favourite activity was getting prepared, the hospital bag was ready by month seven, reading all the paraphernalia—there is soo much that comes with packs and freebie samples. One of my teammates at Oasis came shopping with me at Mothercare. "Go white," she said, "so you can boil everything!" Made sense.

One very rock-solid memory of mine was during this time; Brody took me out for lunch on a Sunday. I had a craving for Spaghetti Bolognaise. I was dropping in at Oasis first and he was going to meet me there, at a good old-fashioned Italian restaurant in our town. We had had a recent discussion about being on time as he was extremely prone to keeping people waiting which drove me crazy. However, he arrived on time well, within five minutes which was really good for him. We had a lovely lunch and I happily tucked into my pasta. After lunch, we took a slow stroll to get back to the car. Our town is on a river and one of the little roads that leads down to the river has a slipway to drive trailers down to let boats into the water. It was a well-known place for cars parking and then getting swallowed by the river when the tide came in.

As we walked closer to this spot, I spied what seemed to be the roof of my car peeking out from the river. The tops of the windows were visible by about 30cm. He had parked there to be on time. It was one of those surreal moments. Was that really my car? I looked at him out of the corner of my eye to see what sort of reaction he was having. Slowly, he said, "FaHkin' 'ell."

I could see him taking in the scene of the drowned car, the small crowd gathering around it, some laughing, some looking worried. I decided to say nothing, absolutely nothing. Creating a scene was not an option. Highlighting to the crowd that it was our car, and he was responsible was also completely out of the question. When we reached the side of the slipway, we stopped and then both very slowly moved on. There was nothing we could have done. I tried to remember if there was anything of value in the car and couldn't. I remained calm and quiet.

'I needed to park quickly ovverwise I knew I'd be gettin' it in ve neck from you about not bein' on time,' was the only explanation and comment I received. Absolutely no apology. It wasn't his fault it was mine for 'moanin' about keeping people waiting, I correctly interpreted. First thing Monday morning, I contacted the insurers and explained the situation. My poor little car was hauled out of the slipway and delivered to the flat. It was of course a write-off and nothing in there survived. They paid out a small sum though and we bought a new little car. In his name.

Before I knew it, five months had passed. The plan was to work until the end of month eight and Victoria would kick in as acting General Manager and then we would assess the situation post-birth. Before that though, I wanted to test the breakfast market so I was opening Oasis for coffees, croissants and bacon rolls at 8 am. I needed to be there ten minutes earlier to switch on the coffee machine and set up with one other of the team. Brody would drop me in 'his' new car, then he would drive on to his office several suburbs away. Most days, he would work in the morning, go to the gym around lunchtime, return to shower and then go out to meet clients for a late lunch, late afternoon or early evening meetings.

Sometimes he would come to Oasis; sometimes, go up to town. We were now in 2001 and mobile phones had become more widely used. Normal. But not for Brody. He refused to conform to the phone fad and he got around the communication barriers by using the phone belonging to whoever he was with. A lot of the time it was mine. Slowly, a new pattern emerged which I was aware of at the time, I just didn't see anything other than we were operating as a unit. He would drop me off at work always three to five minutes late (I am a huge stickler for time and cannot stand being late especially when I am setting an example); then he would drive off, with my mobile phone as I was contactable on the Oasis landline all day not needing it.

Looking back, of course, I see the pattern emerging. The dithering around to delay setting off purposefully, in order to make me late, giving me my phone for a couple of minutes to 'let' me check it before handing it back, the transfer of ownership of the car. Control. If I needed the car, I had to ask for it. If I wanted to keep my phone, I had to ask. And I was vastly out of my comfort zone being late every day. Even though it was only by three to five minutes. It was almost as if it was timed. He knew I could not bear it.

One day, after some exasperation on being late to work consistently, I confronted him and asked why he couldn't build in an extra five minutes to his routine so that I could be on time. He said, "You've boss—you don 'ave ta be on time."

But I wanted to be and surely that was my choice?

What was that all about? My work hours had not affected him in the least in the past nor did my hands-on, side-by-side management approach. In fact, he used to love that. Proudly, he used to call me a soldier. What was making him inflict this little unnecessary yet constant thorn in my side?

One day, I got up early and walked to work—why I didn't simply take the car, I can only understand now. It was the consequences. The threads of control were firmly being sewn.

If I had taken the car, it would have been followed by a couple of days of the silent treatment, and when you have anyone, especially a 120kg person ignoring you in your own home, it is extremely oppressive, heavy on your soul, this would then probably break with, "You're a FAHkin cuNt but I luv ya, Lee and it is goin' ta be alrih'yt. Ya lucky. No one could love you like I do," whilst giving me a big bear hug and kissing my face. At this point, the **relief** would be mental and physical for me.

The pattern which was ever so slowly starting to form is crystal clear only now, looking back. On these types of occasions, I'd be worn down to the point of pure gratefulness to get back to normal, which, I still perceived was life without tension. I was so excited about our little family and the good times still outweighed the bad; in fact, I never even thought about it in those terms. I just remember believing it was all still a mutual learning curve in the next era of our relationship.

I had heard many conversations; in fact, been part of some in Oasis about couples having to work at things, learning to compromise and accommodating certain traits that were different to their own so I thought it was normal on the few occasions I actually reflected on it.

What I question now is, **why**?

Why was the dynamic changing? He fell in love with me because I was independent, hard-working and we had fun. Did falling pregnant make him want me to be dependent on him? I have no idea. I still don't have the answers to this day. Perhaps, it was quite simply just him, sbconscious throwbacks from his life experiences. Insecurities from being left by his parents and spurned by those he loved.

Despite the slowly changing conditions, and they were so so slow, we were both extremely excited about the birth of our baby. He loved it when I was preparing the baby's room. I hand painted the characters of Winnie The Pooh all over one of the yellow walls and made a mobile to hang over the cot with the soft toys that his son had collected over the time we had been together from McDonald's Happy Meals. We liked the same names. James or Cleo. We also both continued to agree not to find out the baby's gender before he or she came out. The surprise was a big thing for both of us. Hence the yellow walls!

I was a very pregnant bridesmaid for one of the besties from the ski season. She and her husband had the most beautiful winter wedding. Velvet and candles and us two bridesmaids wore luxurious green silk and velvet dresses with massive green velvet pashmina-type wraps. I was so excited; it was my first time being a bridesmaid and the three of us were very close plus I loved her husband. He was cool. Still is. The day before, we three had travelled up to the venue to get organised, have an early night and be ready for a bright and early start. I was seven months pregnant at this stage and snored my way through the night.

O, myy godd. My poor friends.

I was a snorer anyway so times that by seven months pregnant and it is bad! Most nights, during our ski season, one of them who drew the short straw of sleeping under me on the bottom bunk would wedge both feet under my mattress and toss me in the air to move my position in the hope of shutting me up! Anyway, we arose on the day of the wedding excited and I got away with a bit of banter. Before we knew it, we were behind the bride at the picture-perfect church which glistened in the healthy sprinkling of snow that had fallen overnight. It was all so beautiful. I fervently looked for Brody. He is not difficult to miss but I definitely couldn't see him from the vestibule. He must be at the end of a pew out of sight, I thought. He was there, he promised, promised, promised, me.

He wasn't.

After the service, we walked back down the aisle and there he was on the last pew on his own. He must have snuck in at some point. I was soo disappointed. Outside though, I didn't get the apology or big kiss and cuddle I was expecting which would have soothed my bubbling emotions. Instead, I got an aggressive thin-lipped, even angry, greeting, on the attack.

"If ya gunna give me a faHkin' hard time you can fucking shah 'up now. The journey here was SHITE and where are ya mean ta faHkin' park in ve middla nowhere?" And then, I heard myself say, "Oh god, I'm sorry. Sounds shit. No hard time. I was just disappointed when I couldn't see you."

Jesus, I was apologising. I was obviously extremely keen not to have a scene; however, I genuinely felt it was my fault he'd had such a rough journey. My reaction was infused to make the situation better for him. Surely that's normal? He was there because of me...

Whilst I was pregnant with Jim, I received two excellent pieces of advice. The first was to listen to all the advice that was coming about how to be pregnant, give birth and then raise a child, even from those who had never had children (as these people are suddenly experts!) and then, do my own thing. Follow my gut and if in doubt, ask a trusted friend who had already trodden the parent path.

The second was to make time for yourselves, to be together regularly in order to keep the original identity you have as a couple. So, I pre-organised exactly that. One of my teammates at Oasis was obsessed with babies. She was a natural with them. I booked her every Thursday just before 7 pm and she would read and put Jim to bed whilst I freshened up and went out to meet Brody locally for a few drinks and some supper. This turned out to be a relationship saver as his evening entertaining clients didn't stop—I had often joined them in the past because they were at Oasis or nearby. Despite my graduation of circumstances to motherhood, his routine remained firmly the same. I am not sure I was expecting any different. I am not sure that I had given it any thought. He was working and I was happy with Jim plus returning to work in some format was lurking and I had to have a plan. However, I was still a little raw from I the night before Jim's due date, Brody was out. There had not been any signs that he was on his way into the world and I wasn't particularly bothered that Brody was out; he was only several miles away but I did assume that he would come home at a reasonable hour.

By 5 am, he was still out! I couldn't help feeling a bit let down. I decided not to try ringing him, (he had my phone) but I took my hospital bag, left a note saying 'Gone into labour' on the steps and went for a drive. I couldn't help myself. It was a beautiful May morning. I allowed myself a little gleeful feeling. I drove to the hospital, a big loop around the local park got a coffee from the early kiosk and sat for a bit contemplating. What would greet me?

Well, it was a very apologetic Brody. This reaction reassured me that he had meant no harm or ill will, simply just carried away with the night. I totally forgave him. It only took one sorry. He had got home, seen the note and called the hospital which of course had no record of me checking in. He had then had visions of me giving birth in the car on the side of the road. I think the shock or worry gave him some sort of rational perspective and he behaved accordingly.

Thank goddddd.

Jim arrived nearly two weeks late at about 1 am in the local hospital. I had been to the doctor who looked at me and said, "You are very big!" quite possibly due to the four stones, I had amassed by then. He made a call and booked me in for an inducement the next day. A Saturday. Brody would be free. Excited doesn't nearly come close to my reaction. Meeting this little person was so close. I got home and rang Brody, from the landline. We decided to meet in Oasis, let them all know and eat there before getting an early night. If I could ever, ever fall asleep! One of the regulars said to me as a parting quip, "Good luck, Jen. It is a lot harder getting them out than getting them in!"

I'm not sure I had actually thought about that in the necessary detail.

Chapter 6
The Newborn Haze

Brody was brilliant during the whole labour/birth process which was quite a long affair. I was given a small private room where I semi-unpacked the long awaited, very patient hospital bag and received instructions on what being induced was all about as well as the process. It was early, around 8.30 am and the first dose was quick to be inserted. I had to lie there for a little while and then walk around. Brody stayed with me until the early afternoon when still nothing seemed to be happening. We then decided it would be a good time for him to pop over and see his son for an hour and then come back. It was actually our weekend to have him and I knew he was excited to hear some news.

Whilst Brody was gone my assigned nurse examined me and it was decided a second dose would probably be needed as there was no movement in terms of dilation or waters broken. It had been eight hours now. He didn't want to come out. My sister, back for a stint, sat with me until Brody returned by which point I was definitely getting some cramps. Then suddenly the frequency increased yet after a further look, I was only three centimetres dilated. Brody and I kept walking and went for a cuppa and a Kit Kat. On the way back, I threw up. He soothed my back and held my hair.

"Vat must be ve pain, darlin'. Let's get 'em to check ya again."

Yup, I was suddenly 9mm dilated. I really wanted an epidural however the nurse was trying to explain to me that 9mm was too far gone. I begged. He begged. There is something about a very large, powerfully strong man pleading with you for a woman in pain. She found an anaesthetist who was still on the ward who would do it.

Thankkkkk god!

I was able to take a breath from the pain and recharge before working with the contractions. In we went to the delivery room and a couple of hours later, I pushed our bubba out whilst holding very tightly onto Brody's hand.

He was exquisite. Healthy. Perfect. A new love affair began.

We had one more night in the hospital for monitoring reasons. Me, not Jim. A few friends and family visited before we went home. My dad was the first with my sister which was reassuring, then the besties from skiing. Brody arrived the next day with his son, whose reaction was just lovely, carrying a car seat for Jim and took us all home. Getting back felt great. We had a lovely day. It was a bank holiday, warm and sunny. Introducing Jim to his room we had spent so long getting ready was wonderful. All his little clothes were folded neatly. Baby paraphernalia, lotions and potions. He looked so incredibly small in his cot. It is a funny thing the size of babies when they emerge.

To the mother who has been carrying them around inside, they feel reasonably big; well, Jim did to me; he was eight pounds four ounces but all my babies did, albeit being a tad smaller. However, to others, they seem so tiny which of course, they are! The day after we got home was a normal working day and Brody, his son, family and friends all went back to work and their lives. For me, it was a heady mix of the amazement of motherhood, getting to know Jim and following my gut as to what to do. Victoria put an A board outside Oasis on the pavement with 'It's a boy!' written in chalk with blue balloons attached to it.

The flowers and gifts streamed in. It was a wonderfully surreal time.

The first reality check was on day three. I hadn't left the flat yet. I had written a couple of thank yous and wanted to whizz them down to the post-box on the corner. Right. So for a three-minute job, I obviously had to take Jim with me. That meant tussling with the baby sling which in itself took at least three minutes! The responsibility started sinking in. The second thing that hit me was that I was literally all alone. I'd had one visitor, my stepmum. She had come after work the night before.

Brody had a normal week's work diary, and we saw him fleetingly in the morning if we were awake as well as for a shower before his afternoon/evening meetings. Mmmm. On day five, I was stir-crazy. I called my sister, and we decided to go out for some dinner at my favourite little Italian. I put Jim in a clean cute jumpsuit, got myself showered and presentable and drove down to the restaurant. It was so good to be out! One small problem however was that Jim wrapped up in his transportable car seat on the seat next to me became hungry too. I was solely breastfeeding still and felt extremely self-conscious. My sister suggested that I pop back to the car give him a feed and she would order. But he was a hungry baby and the ten minutes in the car didn't do it for him. We ended up taking our food home where I could sit and breastfeed in private.

Sole breastfeeding lasted three weeks. I ventured out more and more, getting comfy with it being me and Jim. I took him to see a dear friend of my mum's about an hour out in the countryside. How lovely it was to be with a close friend of hers. The only memory I had of my Mum with little people other than us, was a couple of weeks before her death with a two and half year old. The daughter of our au pair who has very much become part of the family. Mum had been so natural with her. It was a memory I was glad to capture.

Anyway, I was breastfeeding Jim out in the countryside that day and my mum's friend said to me, "You will find it very tricky getting him onto a bottle the longer you leave him on the boob. It is not a bad idea to try getting him on both, plus formula tops up their tummies and you might find he sleeps longer."

Well, firstly, that was a challenge, and I rise to challenges every time! Secondly, he was a big bubba and if he was going to follow Brody in terms of physique then he was only going to get hungrier! That night, I unpacked the bottles, sanitiser, formula and went about preparing a small bottle of milk. The thing was, which now seems very funny, the whole sanitising part wasn't very clear to me. I didn't realise it was sanitation in terms of the milk and formula. I thought it was sanitation of general germs. So, I found tongs and steamed a cloth to wipe down the bottle so I didn't leave a spec of my prints on it or from the kitchen surface. Blimey what a palava. Anyway, I fed him holding the bottle with the steamed cloth. Surely, this wasn't right. I was positive I'd seen people feeding their babies with bottles held by their bare hands. I just hadn't ever taken that much notice.

Jim didn't take to it that night, but he did the following night and then I went to my pre-birth group and floated my exasperation at the sanitising thing! I got a few confused or 'weirdo' looks then one of the ladies explained it was just sterilising from the powdered formula preventing *Cronobacter infection.*

The relief that I didn't have to go through that rigmarole was mixed with feeling a wee bit stupid! Honestly, if my mum had been looking down or hanging around, she would have been thinking 'What the bloody hell **is** she doing…?'

Jim, the good bubba that he was, was sleeping through the night at six weeks. Which meant that I had full nights sleep which puts a different slant on life and clears the new born haze.

Every year, Brody had a tradition of going to Corfu for five days to visit his friend Spiros. They had been to college together and had remained good friends with a penchant for a bit of a party, in common. His annual visit was imminent after Jim's birth six weeks later. He really wanted us both to join him. He booked us into The Corfu Palace. I'm not really sure why he wanted us to join their annual knees up so badly. It was definitely a boy's trip. Another mate of theirs from the rugby scene was joining us who was equally always up for 'good time' but I thought it would be fun, a change of scene plus some sunshine and The Corfu Palace was very very nice. So, Jim's first plane trip was when he was six weeks old. He slept through the whole thing. He was soo good.

On the first day after a late and delicious breakfast, Brody, his rugger bugger friend and Spiros were at the pool bar. I was going to join them after getting Jim and I ready. My friend who had given me the advice about listening to everyone and then doing your own thing had said to me that Jim was too young for sun creams and lotions.

"Just keep him out of the sun **at all times** and simply in a nappy with one of the light baby muslins to tuck him up. And, remember babies drink water as well as milk, especially in the heat." I had borrowed a Moses basket from the accountant at Oasis in which he still looked so small. I on the other hand, in my swimsuit felt so large and never before so self-conscious. Jim and I got to the door of the hotel that led to the pool. Ah. There was no cover from the sun in between the door and the poolside.

The Moses basket was open. I was suddenly aware of his fresh newborn skin and the blistering Greek sunshine. Shit. I stood at the door thinking about a plan of action when a lady probably in her late fifties came and stood by my side.

"Do you need any help?" She asked me. Taking in the Moses basket and seeing Jim. "Ahhh gorgeous. You're brave! How old is he?"

"Thank you. Six weeks." I said honestly wondering what she meant. They had babies in Greece, didn't they? But I was very relieved by the offer and explained my hesitancy.

She lightly covered Jim from head to toe with the muslin and said, "You'll be in the sun for under 30 seconds. You'll be fine. I'll walk with you."

I gathered up the handles of the basket and together we walked the 30-second path to the pool and the bar where Brody and the boys were on the beers. I was extremely thankful to that lady. It was as if she gave me a shot of confidence in a moment when I realised that…on a rare occurrence, my self-assurance faltered.

It was a fun week. Brody had organised a babysitter for the evenings so we could have adult-only dinners. Jim sleeping through the night 7 pm till 7 am meant both Jim and I were getting a decent night's sleep plus he and I grabbed a mid-afternoon siesta together leaving the boys to have man time! My freckles came out. Brody reassured me I would lose my baby weight soon and that I was still gorgeous which fed my weak self-assurance boosted by the fact that I enjoyed dressing up a bit for dinner. We were all happy. Five nights flew. On the last night, we were drifting off to sleep after another delicious meal, feeling full and dreamy, Jim just next to us in his cot.

"You'll neva leave me will ya, Lee?" He said seemingly out of nowhere.

This melted my heart. Leave him? Why would I leave him? We had just started our little family. "Of course not." I said. I was a bit bewildered as to where that had come from.

It was insecurity manifested by most of the people he had loved and held dear, hadin fact, allleft him.

His mum and dad left him with his grandmother.

His grandfather had abandoned the family for his new younger version of his grandmother His uncle and grandmother sided together against him over family money.

His first wife left him taking his son and wanted to move to the other side of the world. No wonder. Well, I was determined that we were creating a new pattern. A new family environment where we had a united front, and we stuck together.

Determined. Plus first and foremost, I had promised I would never leave him and I **absolutely meant it.** We started planning my imminent 30th birthday, together with Jim's christening and our engagement celebrations.

Chapter 7
My Little Family

Obviously, we had to have the party at Oasis. What a day. So much fun. Friends from all over and the gifts for all three celebrations were plentiful. There were speeches, dancing and merriment.

By now, I had been easing back into work two days a week. A bit early at two months according to some, but as you would expect, I completely ignored that chatter. Obviously, I needed help with Jim for this to happen. Our cleaner introduced us to her friend Lena, who had just arrived from one of the South American countries and was looking for work. She had four children of her own who she had left back in her country with her husband. The youngest was four years old. She was desperate to provide a better life for them by working here and sending back money every month. Her day started at 5 am. She would clean offices first and then get to us at 9.30 am (which took an hour) then I would get to work 10 am to 5 pm and her day would finish at 9 pm post her third job cleaning another premises.

We were so blessed to have her. She was amazing on every level. She would lovingly iron Jim's tiny clothes, keep the flat clean and tidy, take him out and play with him, it was almost as if she poured all the love that she couldn't on her own four, onto Jim. I loved her; so did Jim. She would have him by the window just before 5 pm so he and I could see each other as I walked up the road towards home. She was my rock at home. Our weekly routine formed a structure. Mondays, the weekly reports were rang into me; Tuesdays and Wednesdays, I worked; Thursday night was date night; Friday, I took Jim for lunch at Oasis. Brody came and went on his own schedule as he always had.

I was in heaven and addicted to motherhood. It was like a drug. I fell pregnant again a month later. Brody had encouraged me not to bother going back on the pill. Why bother? I wanted another baby so let's crack on. Four months after Jim had popped out, Cleo was on her way although again we chose not to find out the sex. When I told my dad, he looked at me for what felt just a bit too long. Why did he need to work at being happy for me? I knew what I was doing.

The trips away were high on Brody's agenda. Rome was next. My dad and stepmum were up for having Jim for the weekend which was amazing. My stepmum although a little unsure was really up for it. Who would have thought? Whilst I was still pregnant with Jim, I had asked her what she wanted to be called by her grandkids. She chose Nonna. Italian for grandmother.

So, Jim went off to Grandad and Nonna's with copious notes and provisions and we went off to Rome to stay at The Grand. It was indeed extremely grand. Our suite was luxurious and came with a butler. We walked the streets of Rome hand in hand with a personal guide organised by our butler, who led us to a hidden restaurant full of Italians, no tourists. I truly felt I was living the dream. I had a bubba growing; one safe with my parents whilst we were having quality time together in Rome no expense spared. Life was great. Our guide sat with us in her favourite café, buzzing with the locals drinking little cups of espresso's in swift sips before resuming their morning. She spotted my slightly swollen tummy and asked when the baby was due. I then asked her if she had any children. She told us that six months earlier she had given birth to twin girls two months premature. Neither of the tiny babies survived. She and her husband had held a funeral for their daughters who were unable to survive more than 24 hours regardless of the efforts of the hospital team. They were just not cooked enough. I was deeply affected by this story not able to begin to imagine the horrific emotions and the act of burying a child let alone two at the same time. Utterly brutal. I wanted to wrap my arms around her when I said how sorry I was. It made me realise how lucky I was, and that you just never know what life is going to throw at you.

Whilst I was pregnant with Cleo and Jim was around eight months old, I had a yearning to live in a house with a garden. I felt we needed to move forward on the property front too and the investment slant would persuade Brody to move. He was very set in his ways, reluctant to uproot, he liked being settled with all his stuff around him. The buyout of my brother and sister still left us having a decent amount of joint equity in the flat to access as a deposit. So, I suggested we keep and rent the flat. It was still in my name. He thought it the most efficient for tax purposes to keep his name off ownership documents.

Thankkk goddd.

Little did I know that this didn't even scratch the surface of his reference to 'efficiencies'. More of that maybe another time. Anyway, I found the perfect house. A smaller neighbouring town still walking distance to Oasis, close to the river with parks and playgrounds plus, for when the time came, schools with good reputations. It had a little garden and three bedrooms with additional space in a semi-converted loft which was perfect for a spare bed, Brody's desk and rowing machine. He orchestrated the finances. We took out as much equity as possible from the flat and managed to rent it for enough to cover the new increased monthly mortgage payments. Bingo. We packed up and moved in.

Lena was now coming to us three days a week and the wife of the chef at Oasis did an afternoon/night so I had at least one evening shift on duty. It was important for me to see the regulars plus the place was going from strength to strength. Breakfasts had taken off and we were capitalising on every possible minute to open, including the launch of the Oasis Sunday Roast which we made family friendly.

I had introduced little things to set Sunday apart like linen napkins, posh salt and pepper shakers and wiki sticks to amuse the kids. A slightly different targeted clientele to the norm. Had I orchestrated this because I was growing a family? I was becoming the target market. Quite possibly. I hadn't initiated it before! Either way, the shareholders were happy. Profits were gently going in the right direction year on year, so they repaid me by being incredibly flexible as a new working mum. Pregnant again!

Cleo's pregnancy flew by. Not surprisingly really. I was nesting in a new home, had a baby turning one and had a busy bar to run. I felt on top of the world.

We had been in the new house for about two days, littered with boxes, we still had some of my siblings' things, mine,

Jim's of course and all of Brody's, he wouldn't let me throw anything out, not one little thing. That evening, I mentioned one of the besties and her husband (I was her very pregnant bridesmaid) were popping round. Brody was on his way out. He stopped still in the hallway.

"No FAHkin WAY," he roared.

Stunned, I halted what I was doing and turned to look at him. He had on his thin-lipped, aggressive 'try me' face. What the fuck was this reaction?

"You carn av anyone roun'ere til all vis is sorted an pu' away an evry box fla uned an given back to va movers. No fucker commin roun ere wiv vis faHkin mess." His eyes were wide, eyebrows up.

What? I am not sure I had heard anything quite so ridiculous. Made even more so by the fact that he hadn't unpacked anything at all except his desk stuff.

I laughed.

I couldn't help myself it was so ludicrous. The best yet. How would I even articulate that to my friend? 'Sorry, you can't come round after all because **I** haven't unpacked all the boxes yet.' She would laugh just as much and possibly even question my sanity. Definitely question my sanity. However, laughing was absolutely the wrong move.

He faced me full-on as a response. His top lip became even thinner, his eyes hard and wide, almost as if he was going into battle. My laugh stopped mid 'ha' and I took in the scene almost from an outer body perspective. Not good. My senses told me to placate and reassure him immediately. Something had obviously rattled him. What the fuck that was god only knew but now was not the time to explore exactly what.

"I'm sorry. I'm so sorry, I didn't mean to make you angry. Of course. That's fine, I will re-arrange them for when it is all clear." I said and with that, hanging in the air his face relaxed and he left, quietly closing the door. I stood speechless looking at the closed door. Our new 'Welcome' mat lay at the foot. What to do? They were due in about 30 minutes; possibly, had already left. Shit. I couldn't cancel them. I just couldn't. What would I say? The whole thing was so strange.

What on earth had kicked off a reaction like that? What had I done?

Doing something with other people without him? People that he probably sensed didn't approve. New house jitters? He had moved twice in 18 months. A lot for someone who couldn't stand moving. He had moved for me.

I took the gamble that he would be out for at least two hours, possibly three. My friends arrived. It was so good to see them; for some reason, it had been a while. I showed them around the house dodging the boxes with Jim on my hip. She was his god mum and felt comfy taking him for a little while and helping with his supper. They were there for an hour when I felt myself feeling on edge. For me, Brody's anger remained tangible and for their sake as well as mainly my own, they needed to go. This was so unlike me. Usually, I'd be opening up the wine, getting out nibbles and chatting for hours sometimes I'd end up making supper or ordering in, especially as I hadn't seen them for ages. But what if he came back? I started murmuring about doing bath and bed and how tired I was. My friend picked up on the hint immediately.

"No problem, Jen," she said, "we'll be off. School night and we're both up early doors."

I looked at her sending silent thank you's for being so intuitive and just going with it as only a very best friend can. Big hugs followed and off they went. I didn't see her for another five months until Cleo was born. One of my best friends who lived five miles away.

Brody's comeback to that little episode was to focus on a summer holiday for us all after Cleo was born. Where would I like to go? My mother's absence was bordering on excruciating as I was exploring being a mother myself. Our last holiday with her had been in Majorca up in the north. The three of us with Mum and our Nana. We didn't realise at the time but Mum was on her last legs. In fact, she died three weeks after we got back having gone straight to the hospital from the airport. Those two weeks together in Majorca were a very special time in a place that became as equally special to us three siblings. I really wanted to go back.

"Of course, darlin', anywhere ya like. She would have loved me, ya mum, wouldn she?"

Would she? Yes, I'm sure she would have. His laugh, generosity. Anyway, I booked a two-week holiday in the same hotel that we'd stayed in with Mum. I took a punt that this baby was going to be a little late too and booked for when I thought she would be seven to eight weeks old. I was so comforted that this was looming that I set about nesting. I did indeed unpack all the boxes with Lena's help. I sorted out Jim's room and then set about preparing the new baby's little room. I had it painted purple this time and hooked up the McDonald's toy mobile above the cot. I was soo excited. My second bubba was on the way. Even Jim's birth experience, the pain, did nothing to quell the bubbles of elated emotion I was carrying. My little family was growing.

Cleo arrived on my birthday. Now, our birthday. Talk about a cherry on top. I loved that. Plus, the hospital gave us a private ensuite for the night we stayed because of it. She had been two weeks late but shot out when the time came. Brody had dropped me and popped back to the office for an hour as we had thought that judging by Jim's long labour it would be a while.

However, they had given me the inducement gel, I'd had a warm bath and then felt contractions almost immediately. The nurse had given me some pethidine which must have accelerated the process somehow because suddenly she was coming. Brody arrived back just in time to help get me in a wheelchair and into the labour room. Out she came. The midwife who had this calming yet commanding Jamaican lilt guided me through the pushing. She was absolutely wonderful. I was still high from the pethidine as I was wheeled out and called back to her, "I'll be back next year." As I looked adoringly down at my little daughter, I was also high on motherhood.

She was actually only eight weeks old when Brody, his eldest son, Jim, Cleo and I set off for Majorca. The local people we had met on the holiday with Mum were still around. Their familiarity and conversations about her were extremely comforting. I felt her all around us. The hotel manager had a niece who was up for babysitting quite a few of the nights. So, I would do supper, bath and put Cleo down and she would play with Jim for a bit before putting him to bed. This meant that Brody, his son and I would have dinner together. It was a wonderful holiday. Technically, I was on maternity leave; however, I was in close contact with Victoria. Oasis was in its quiet season.

One night, Brody's son stayed with the little ones and the babysitter whilst Brody took me out for dinner at the charming five-star hotel across the water at the northernmost tip of the island. This hotel coincidentally was his grandfather's favourite holiday spot and Brody had happy memories of visiting him there. It was special because of its refined, understated elegance no bling in sight, at all. I felt very comfortable there whilst obviously being very spoilt. There was a terrace that led down to the sea with bougainvillea the light purple flowered climber at every turn and in the evenings tiny lights paved the way. The restaurant was on a big balcony overlooking the terrace and the water at its edge. Every table was by the balustrade, so everyone had the view. The food was exquisite, to die for as was the very expensive wine he ordered in abundance. So there we were just the two of us enjoying every second. These moments were wonderful. He had my undivided attention. I made him proud because I was dressed up and looking good. I had only put on two stone with Cleo's pregnancy and had lost a lot of the surplus already having learnt my lesson from Jim's! Brody was spending his money on everything he loved. He was calm, loving, funny. I was getting a strong shot of who I fell in love with. We got to dessert.

"I know you wan' anova baby, you wanna have free like your lot so less just get on wif it," he said. "I wanna make you 'appy, Lee, an' I can see ya well mummed up. Lovin' it, aintchya?" This was true. So true.

"'Appy when ya pregnant an' 'appy when ya wif ya bubbas—our bubba's that I'm given ya."

Now this would probably make some people's hair stand on end but I knew it was just Brody's style. His way of reinforcing the 'us' as well as a gentle reminder he was giving me, providing me with what I wanted. A family. He very much wanted that too. A secure family unit where no one left. I totally got that and I felt that I was helping provide that for him, in return. A united front?

I completely forgot about the strange, controlling situations that were beginning to increase in occurrence. I didn't question the why on why they were happening either. I just knew he was different, and I loved him. Other couples had their 'things'. Relationships just can't be perfect all of the time.

So, we decided that I wouldn't go back on the pill and we'd see what happened. Nothing happened. For a little while.

We kicked into a routine on return in our new place. Lena was thrilled at having another baby in the house. She was amazing and both Jim and Cleo loved her. Another piece of advice that I picked up from a friend who was a nanny to a high net-worth family was, 'Don't ever let jealousy grip you if your children love their nanny. Embrace it. Having someone they love and want to be with is a blessing that is rare and often never achieved.' So, I loved her too. Because they loved her did not mean they loved me any less. I was wonderfully comfortable with the fact that I was my children's most favourite person in the whole wide world. This was a constant Ready Brek feeling.

Oasis continued to do well. Victoria was in her element as my right-hand woman and whilst I didn't physically spend the same amount of time there my mind was on the job most of the time. I did a lot of the admin from home so that when I was there I was visible, working the floor and bantering with the customers, not stuck in the office. The shareholders were happy because of the numbers and feel of the place. Jim, now one and a half loved being in there. He knew he would get his favourite food from the kitchen, and he found pressing the buttons on the soft drink gun hilarious when the bubbly liquids poured out. I felt happy in control and still highly engaged in my career. The majority of my salary went on our mortgage, household expenses and childcare. This did two things. Gave me the feeling that I was substantially contributing however it left me with very little expendable income which meant of course I had to ask Brody for spending money and children's activity costs. Initially, this seemed like an effective game plan.

Brody was on to our next trip. Just the two of us. We were off to Venice staying at the Gritti Palace for Valentine weekend. This time, Jim was off to stay with friends whose two boys Lena looked after on the days that she wasn't with us, so she was going to be there the first day to settle him in and Cleo was off to very close friends, actually Jim's god dad whose wife was one of my confidants at the time. They had three children and she would have had more but decided to stop for various reasons. She was the one, who told me that I would get advice of all sorts and to listen, take it on board and then do my own thing. She was soo right.

So, the weekend arrived. I was very excited. Cleo was six months and we hadn't had a night to ourselves without the kids since Rome. When I got back from work I packed up the car with all paraphernalia or both kids, travel cots, buggy, clothes, nappies, favourite teddies and notes f on them both. Anything to make everybodies lives as easy as possible for the three nights we were away. Brody came home and put his feet up. I then drove the two-hour round trip to drop them off. Leaving Cleo was a little more difficult than I thought. Her cute little face with big eyes watched me whilst sitting in my friend's arms, bringing in all her stuff and setting up the cot. When it was time to go, I felt the sting of tears, noticed by my friend. She said, "We are going to have a fun weekend and so are you, off you go. Just turn around and walk out the door. Quickly."

I got back home. Brody hadn't moved. Empty crisp packets and a pint of squash were on the coffee table. What the fuck?

I was on the cusp of saying something along the lines of…

"You ok? It has just taken me over three hours to load, deliver and say goodbye to our children whilst you've sat with your fucking feet up the entire time. What the fuck are you doing? Thanks a fucking lot."

But knowing what would absolutely follow, I decided it was not worth ruining our lovely trip to Venice potentially peppering the experience with verbal abuse and silent treatment. It was almost like he knew what I wanted to say. Almost taunting me to try it. I focused on packing and the treat that was one sleep away.

The Gritti Palace was unbelievable. Where the Grand in Rome had been completely ostentatious, gold, bling and butlers, The Gritti was pure class. A restored former noble home, it sits on the Grand Canal with views of the Santa Maria Church. A very special place.

After a private launch whisked us over the water from the airport and dropped us off at the hotel, we kicked off with Bellini's in Harry's Bar. As usual, there was no expense spared. We had two full days and walked around Venice both mornings finding terrific lunch spots and enjoying long leisurely meals before slowly venturing back to the hotel. We decided that we wouldn't risk getting Brody into a gondola although enjoyed watching the rigmarole of it with other tourists. A fascinating city and a truly wonderful experience. I felt the united front reinstated and solid. I fell pregnant.

Chapter 8
The First Pang of Hate...

Of course, I felt pregnant fantastic. Physically. This was my lucky theme. Plus knowing a third chick was on the way gave me the Ready Brek feeling. My family was completing. The pregnancy went really fast. I was on a roll. My home, my routine enabled me to fit in just enough time for being a working mum without feeling I was missing out on the kids. However, it felt that our Thursday nights were holding us together. Brody continued to come and go on his own schedule which was fine yet it was dawning on me that when I wanted to go out, I had to organise a babysitter and bypass him. But, unless this was work-related, it irritated Brody very much. In fact, it felt that I irritated him a lot if I strayed in any way from routine when it didn't involve him. He liked to know where I was, what I was doing and who I was with. At all times.

By the time our summer holiday came around in July, I was five and a half months pregnant. Cleo was just one and Jim, two and two months old. We stayed in the happy place, where I had holidayed with Mum on our last holiday. And what was very exciting was that my brother and sister were joining us on a flying visit, staying with our friends around the corner.

The hotel Illa D'Or is nestled on The Pine Walk with this terrific terrace on the water looking out across the bay to Alcudia. Mountains are the backdrop. There is a little bit of beach which creates this wonderfully safe spot for children to sit and paddle in the water. Over the years, we have spent hours on this terrace and feel very much at home and at peace there. This particular holiday we had Brody's son, now eleven, and with us was our lovely Lena. Our holiday routine was that she would take them after their bath in the evenings and put them to bed and she slept in the same room. I would take over at breakfast, this meant that we could have an adult dinner and a bit of lie-in and she had the days to herself. It worked really well, a treat and I knew it. I was incredibly grateful because it meant we didn't come back from holiday still a bit knackered.

Anyway, early on in the holiday, we had settled on the terrace after breakfast and handover. Jim didn't want to put his arm bands on because of this pretty horrific graze from a cataclysmic fall just before we left. It was all around his elbow, down one arm which was still quite fresh. For a second, I focused on making sure Cleo was completely out of the sun and had some juice which must have taken around thirty seconds. I looked up and caught sight of Jim's little baseball cap in the water with just his eyes visible. He was in trouble. I ran to dive in, tripped in the little sandy area and fell flat on my bump. I scrambled to get up, panicked. Luckily, another mum close by had spotted him too and reached him before I could get up and get to him. She passed him to me and I clutched him in big fat relief sitting on the sand.

It transpired that he, in those thirty seconds had followed his big brother into the water who was himself unaware and diving about. Jim was a little shocked but recovered fast and we went back to Cleo at the table. It was then I heard Brody's belly laugh in sarcastic mode. Sitting at the bar with a cold pint of beer and his first cocktail of the day, he'd watched the whole scene, and had not moved. I looked at him on the brink of tears and he looked straight back at me.

"It's your own faHkin fawl. You shoulda made 'im pu' on the faHkin armbans." He said, slurping on his cocktail.

I can't remember exactly all that I felt at the time. I think immediately, relief was still washing over me that Jim was safe, and I didn't seem to have any repercussions from falling. I sat and hugged them both, him, and Cleo to me.

I believe it was my first pang of hate.

My brother and sister had flown out to stay with our friends and have a couple of days with us on holiday. My sister, over from Australia had not had much time with Cleo and spent as much as possible with the kids. That evening, we were all going out together for supper. I came down to the terrace after handing over the kids to Lena and she was waiting for me, the others had gone ahead.

"Are you ok?" She said, "I heard about the fall today."

"Yes, I'm ok," I replied not wanting to let on any other emotion in case I burst into tears, the whole experience had rocked me.

At the table, somehow, she had ended up sitting next to Brody's son with Brody one up at the head of the table. It all started off quite pleasantly. Small talk, chit-chat about the hotel, how lovely it was to be in the sunshine when we started talking about girlfriends and boyfriends just generally, probably because both she and I had had holiday romances here. Then almost out of the blue, he said, "My sons ain't gunna have no wishy washy birds as girlfrienz."

"Well, it is more important they find someone they like rather than anything else, isn't it?" My sister questioned.

He leaned his mammoth torso on the table via one elbow so his face was as close to her as possible. With the other arm pointed his finger right at her.

"Wha ve faHk do you know?" He replied. " You aven even got a boyfriend. Avnt had one in years." Then, he looked at me and said, "Shu er up or I'll fahk er off." The table went quiet.

"Please," I said, "Please, Brody, don't ruin the evening."

My sister got up, left the table and disappeared into the ladies' loo at the end of the restaurant. I followed. I found her inside with tissues wiping her eyes.

"He is disgusting, Jennie. Fucking disgusting. How can you bear it?" This was the only time, ever, that she was vaguely confrontational about him, us. We three siblings just weren't wired that way.

"I'm so so sorry. I know and I'm truly sorry." I felt sick. How dare he talk to her like that. Where was my sassy take no shit attitude? It just wasn't to hand. I couldn't muster the gumption not just to say something in retaliation but to endure whatever would follow which could possibly last the rest of the holiday. I knew he would prefer to ruin our holiday for me than to accept that he had behaved in any other way than acceptable.

Firstly, she had a point. Secondly, he had behaved really badly. Shitty by anyone's standards. He didn't care. Not one tiny bit.

She went back to the table and sat at the other end close to my brother. It was absolutely awful. Why? Why couldn't he just have a decent adult conversation without antagonising and being so derogatory? This wasn't being united; it was divisive. I wasn't sure what he thought he was achieving with this aggressive, belittling flare-up. His son looked at me with a sad expression. I picked up the conversation again with a new topic, away from family, love, money or any topic that could possibly trigger him off.

Walking back to the hotel that night, I took stock of the day. It had not been a good one. The next day, my brother and sister were off back to England before her onward journey back to Australia. I remember feeling it might be a bit easier after that as Brody wouldn't feel he was sharing me with them. How sad. However, there was finally a spark. It was like a keyhole opening of awareness about the reality of his character. He had watched me fall on my bump, the bump with our bubba inside and the only thing that moved was his hand to get his cocktail to his mouth. And then, he had laughed. This was followed by a completely uncalled-for nasty outburst at my sister which reduced her to tears. All of this in just one day, but on a holiday, normally, our very safe space, I felt a seizure of extreme sadness anchor itself in the pit of my stomach.

The rest of the holiday was a bit of a mixed blur spent happily playing with Jim and Cleo, Brody's son and avoiding anything other than light-hearted conversation with Brody to keep him calm and pleasant. I tried not to delve too deeply into that day, subconsciously mindful of what might come to light. Saying farewell to my siblings was very difficult. Sorrowful, yet I couldn't openly show it, uncertain of what the consequences would be. I gave them both big hugs whilst fighting back the tears. I knew what they were thinking. I was in a horrific situation without a solution that wasn't equally horrific. And that soon, I was going to wake up to it. Harrowing for them.

Back in England, I kicked into a protective routine at home and work whilst counting down the days to meet my third bubba.

Chapter 9
Resorting to Violence

I have thought back often with a fine-tooth comb as to when it all started going so wrong or more aptly, when my eyes began to open, realising the sorry state of affairs which was my life, for what it really was. It was tricky because all the signs were there glaring at me from the very beginning, with hindsight but that day on holiday falling on my bump, was definitely the start of my awakening. Isn't it strange that once you are slightly aware of something, so much more becomes noticeable? For me, it was a cascade.

I started to realise he didn't really have much to do with the kids unless we were in a pub drinking and they were running around the garden. He rarely came to anything at school. He literally existed as a single person dipping in when it suited him. He was extraordinarily selfish. However, in the past, that hadn't bothered me so much during our purple patch when I was in love; after a bolt of realistic awareness, I became slightly indignant which drove more of a wedge between us. This in turn nudged me more into my shell. Head down, get on with it, coming out to engage with him as little as possible. This of course fed his insecurities like kindle to an open fire which in turn increased his nasty, controlling streak. I can see it all now plain as day.

There was an incident that increased the rapidity of the cascade. The four of us were in the car at the flat that was having a lick of paint plus a few other maintenance bits by a newly found efficient polish gent. We pulled up and I went in to check how it was all going leaving the kids and Brody in the car. Magic (Jim couldn't pronounce his name in the Polish version!) our man had discovered a few potential problems which he went through with me. This took about fifteen more minutes than we had planned. As I came out of the flat I saw Brody driving away. Luckily half way down the street the traffic lights turned red for just enough time for me to waddle, catch them up and hop in.

'Where are you going?' I panted.

'Gotta crack on Lee. Wha ve faHk was takin suh long?' He replied.

O myy god you nasty motherfucker I thought as I checked on the kids, thankfully oblivious. The naivety of being two and three on the cusp of expiring.

Another day, we were all together at the front door coming home. I think it was just coincidental that we had arrived home altogether. I was now seven months pregnant and I had Jim and Cleo in the double buggy with multiple bags dangling off it which I'd always promised myself I'd never do. Bag lady, buggy mum, but there I was! Anyway, I couldn't find the front door key immediately.

"'JESUS faHkin christ LEE. What's up wif ya?"

"Brody, just give me a sec and it is not actually ok to talk to me like that." Whilst thinking he could have opened the door for me. He had his keys in his pocket.

"Yea? Well, yu talk to ya staff how you wan. I'm ve boss here so I'll talk to you how I wan."

Ohhh myyyy god. Was I his staff now?

At this point in the big picture, I was still clinging on with every breath to the theme that I was going to hold us together. How could I not? We were expecting our third bubba. What he needed was for me to provide a united front and prove that I was still there for him. That was getting tougher and tougher though. I felt as if every day I was starting afresh with him, having to prove myself in terms of love and commitment. It was as if there was no emotional credit. It was absolutely exhausting. Soon after the front door key episode, he met me in Oasis after a Friday day shift, the idea being that he would pick me up and we would get a big family KFC and take it home for all of us. He had been at a long lunch.

I was driving. We were a couple of minutes from the KFC but stuck in a little bit of traffic.

"'Why ve faHkin 'ell did ya come vis way…?"
Something came over me. It felt like rage but I wasn't sure because I had never felt that way before. I lifted my right foot up and over the gear stick and shoved my heel right into his face three times. There was blood. It felt sooo good. There was this haze around me, I felt all muddled up, exhausted and so angry all at the same time. He got out of the car, slammed the door and came round the bonnet of the car to my door. As soon as I realised what he was doing, I locked the doors and jammed the gearstick into first, nudging him out of the way squeezing down the middle of the road with cars honking at me. I didn't care; I knew I had to get away. I drove home and as quickly as I could, I relieved the Chefs wife and double-locked the front door with the inside latch firmly on. I must

have composed myself well because the kids didn't notice anything about me that was strange, and as it was fairly usual that Brody wasn't there; to them, it must not have seemed any different. I kept breathing as steadily as possible. He did come to the door sometime later, I can't remember exactly how much later; I had put the kids to bed and was sitting on the bottom step wondering what the hell to do.

I knew he would come home but I don't think he thought that I would lock him out. My gut was screaming at my brain not to let him in. I didn't. He tried to open the door, realised that it was double-locked and called my name several times. He seemed pretty calm and I almost relented, but I didn't. There was no one to call, no one to talk to. I couldn't let anyone know what had happened otherwise there would be a crack in the outward perception. I went to bed and tried to get some sleep. I am not sure where he slept that night. I have never ever asked him, probably because I felt that would open up an opportunity to verbally attack me as obviously, it would be my fault he couldn't sleep at home in his own bed. He would never see that my reaction was a result of the constant belittling. However, I felt ashamed. In the cold light of the next morning, I berated myself for losing my cool. Not just losing my cool but resorting to violence.

Oh, myy goooodddd.

Lena, for some reason, was coming that day. A Saturday. I can't remember why but thankfully, she was there.

I decided to call one of Brody's best friends the one that I felt wouldn't judge, knew him, god dad to his eldest son and to Jim. I explained what had happened and that I didn't know what to do. He ended up brokering a meeting at his house. I left Lena with the kids and went round. His wife was the lovely lady who had given me lots of advice and she greeted me with a big hug. He arrived soon after me, entering their kitchen and addressing his friend, "My wife," as he often referred to me, "is a faHkin cunt." This was spat out with a smirk on his face which had been cleaned up but three very angry red marks etched the left side of his nose. Astonishingly, I found myself running into his arms repeating, "I'm sorry," over and over again. He gave me a big hug and said, "Ya lucky, I love ya Lee. You're a CuNt but I love ya. Too much excitement for ve bubba. You af to calm down."

In the car on the way home, he didn't say anything. Silence. Was he not going to say anything at all? What could I say that wouldn't make him blow up? I had this extraordinary feeling of dread mixed with a tiny bit of jubilance. A flash of my old self reappearing? I sort of wanted to say, "Take that, you fucker."

Obviously, I did not. Now that I had opened on the physical front, I was extremely worried that the theme might weave its way into our relationship. He had always had a very negative stand on it. Hitting a girl was not acceptable, in any way shape or form. However he was clearly a little bit rattled from the night before and I have no idea what he would have done if he had managed to get to me and open the driver side door.

"What's your plan today?" I asked tentatively. I didn't know what I wanted him to say. If we went out together and people asked about his face I would have to fess up, take the blame. I wasn't sure I could do that. Jim's vocabulary was limited and Cleo couldn't talk yet so I wasn't too worried about them. I put my hands on my seven-month bump as if to reassure it.

"I'm goin' to va rugby, darlin'." Silence.

Ok, well at least he was out of the house. Usually, I would walk to the rugby ground with the double buggy, Jim and Cleo wrapped up and join him for a few drinks after the game. Jim would get a run around on the pitch and Cleo would be on my hip saying hello to the rugby crew. I didn't know whether it would make him happy for us joining him or not, that day. So I asked him. "Shall we join you after?" What would people say about his face I fretted…

"Yes, darlin' come along." He was glossing over the whole thing. I felt relieved. No talking meant no anger. Which also meant of course nothing was discussed. Nothing was ever explored or mended. I did join him at the rugby that evening. Me and my bump, Jim, Cleo. His face wasn't ever brought up by any of the rugby lot. Who knows what had been said over lunch? Definitely something with that lot. Whatever it was though, it was put to bed and never mentioned to me.

Chapter 10
Django's Arrival

Django's birth was a completely different experience from Jim or Cleo's. It was November and again it felt he was very happy where he was. It got to a week past his due date and the hospital asked me to come in for a 'sweep' to try and get him moving. Nothing. They sent me home. I was tired and just wanted to get on with it all. Plus Jim and Cleo were at my dad and stepmum's but they had said they could only do the day as they had a dinner party that night. So, we went to pick them up and went home. I did bath and bedtime and then sat down with a large glass of wine. I felt tired and emotional which was rare for me. I really wanted him out. I managed to get through to Monday morning when I knew Lena was arriving. I called the hospital and they said they had a room in the Green suite, I could come in and they would induce me.

After about three hours of walking up and down the hospital stairs, labour kicked in! Waters broke. He was coming. The contractions started.

"I'd like to order some pethidine, please," I said to the nurse.

She looked at me, "Ah sorry, sweet, this is the GREEN wing. No drugs."

"You have got to be fucking joking," I said, "that was not explained at all. How am I supposed to know GREEN means drug-free? You have to communicate these things. I'll move to another room, suite, wing, whatever."

"Sorry, sweet, but we are overflowing everywhere else. You'll be fine. You can have some gas and air."

Ohh, myyyyy godddddd.

So it was gas and air. I had to get on with it. I was soo relieved to have something that I nearly passed out after sucking in too much of the gas. Then I felt sick. Then Brody arrived. I vaguely remember him giving encouragement and being close; it was just that the pain was excruciating. The screams of the woman next door filled me with fear. Was I screaming like that? I had no idea. Then he came. My little Django. He was slightly smaller than Cleo; thank god, without any pain relief the smaller the better! How women do childbirth without drugs and keep coming back for more, is a mystery of nature. I guess what you get after the pain provides the amnesia. But we were fine. Healthy and happy and on the usual high!

Brody went home to relieve Lena. Django and I had a small private 'green' room. He was a very happy bubba. That night, he just fed and slept, fed and slept and before I knew it, it was breakfast time and Brody was back to pick us up. We went home to introduce him to Jim and Cleo. Jim was two and a half and Cleo was one year and four months. My little family felt complete but there was this constant nagging thing somewhere in my stomach or was it my mind/subconscious? I never wanted to explore it. I just wanted to be a mumma to my chicks and have a happy family.

Cleo had joined Jim at our local nursery; they were there two days a week. They loved it. It was such a sweet little place run by a husband and wife. They painted, baked, played and put on little performances, the first one for both of them together was the nativity that December.

The usual routine kicked back into place only added to with breastfeeding sessions. I breastfed all my babies for at least five weeks maximum of eight weeks and after the bottle experience with Jim, I got them onto a bottle too after three days. This meant they were always well fed plus it meant that someone else could feed them which is extremely helpful at whatever stage you were at. The one thing Brody didn't mind doing was sitting on the sofa bottle feeding obviously as long as it slotted into his plans for the day. I remember my stepmum coming by after work in those early few weeks and whilst I prepared and fed supper for Cleo and Jim, she was able to sit and chat whilst giving Django a bottle. That's a lovely memory.

On the flip side, one very early morning breastfeed at roughly 3 am, I heard Brody go to the loo which was right next to Django's room. He went straight back to bed. Not even a head round the door to say hi. That made me feel very sad right then, though justifying and brushing it off with 'That's just Brody!' which was part of my normal internal daily dialogue.

Luckily for me, all the children were sleeping through the night at six weeks old. Part of the reason, along with feeling fantastic during pregnancy that fed the motivation to have them in quick succession. Sleep for me is integral. A quick doze here and there has saved me on many an occasion but to only be sleep-deprived for the first six weeks post-giving birth allowed me to have my usual energy back. Enough energy to take on the world and all that Brody brought to it!

When Django was two weeks old, I took the three of them to one of those pottery places where you can decorate a variety of pottery pieces and get them kilned. It is one of my happy memories. We did plates with imprints of all three of their feet. Three little feet with Christmas trees around them. Jim and Cleo giggled as I painted their soles and tried staying desperately still whilst I positioned them on the plates. They were very proud to give them out as Christmas presents. I still have one. That Christmas, the first one as a complete family of six with Brody's eldest son was a good one. I was on maternity again and apart from the odd popping into Oasis over the ten-day Christmas period, I was fully at home. Just where Brody wanted me.

One of my oldest friends, actually our mums were pregnant together, her birthday is on the 5th January. As soon as we recovered from New Year's Day, I have nearly always remembered to get her card in the post. This particular year, I actually had the card ready to write and then post. I was in the sitting room, all the kids milked up and dressed for the day. Brody was in the big armchair with Django nestled in one arm. So sweet. He looked so small against Brody's big frame. I wrote the card, sealed it, got up and said, "I'm just going to pop this in the post. I'll be back in a sec." Brody looked up.

"You'll ave ta take ve kids I'm off ouwt."

"Really? I'll be four minutes maximum five." The post-box was at the bottom of our road.

"Nah. Gotta get ready." With that, he got up, propped Django, now seven weeks old, back in the nook of the chair, went upstairs, shut the bathroom door and turned on the shower.

What the fuck! For god's sake. I couldn't believe it. I should have, because I knew my two-day-a-week physical return to work was looming and I also knew that was a catalyst for his behaviour towards me to deteriorate with actions just like this, that were returning.

I bundled them up into their warm stuff, Django in his all-in-one fluffy cozy thing. Victoria had given the three of them all-in-ones for Christmas. They were very cute. Jim was now on a buggy board behind the double buggy. With everyone in position, we went to post the card. It didn't bother me taking my chicks; it was just the ludicrousness of Brody's reaction. He couldn't give me four minutes? I took it on the chin and packed it away in my subconscious not challenging it, probably for fear of what I would really unearth if I went down that path. As always.

Normal life and with it, routine resumed simply with one more chicken. Django was an exceptionally good baby. Happy to sit and watch his brother and sister. Equally, they were happy to hold his bottle for him and 'gently' well, their form of gently, bounce him on his lounger. On the days that I worked, Brody would drop off the kids, Jim and Cleo to the nursery, then me to work before going off to his work (his parental job done for the day) and Lena would have Django and help wonderfully around the house. It was like clockwork. Thursday nights, Brody and I came together as a couple. It was only ever us, we never included anyone else. We would often stay local on occasion; I would go up more towards the West End to meet him after lunch/meetings. We would talk about work, whatever deal he was working on, friend gossip, the kids, our next trip, sometimes family and sometimes my work unless he felt I wasn't managing something correctly and then he would get vocal.

Whatever the topic, the time together was our time and we always ate well and drank fine wine. Sunday was the only day that we were together as a family. We would often have a roast in the winter months and BBQs in the summer. That first year of Django's life, I felt was good. I was completely wrapped up in my mum heaven whilst having a busy bar to run which provided me with a healthy work life balance not to mention the ability still to pay the mortgage.

That summer, we went to Sardinia. The lovely hotel in Mallorca wouldn't accept our booking which was a bit soul destroying for me given the memories of my mum but deep down I felt it was a small blessing in disguise as memories from the last summer were not good. I knew it was because of him. His attitude to the manager, staff and other guests had been appalling. But I tucked that away. We were seven. Brody's eldest, Jim, Cleo, Django, and Lena. Our hotel was lovely. Right on the beach. Staying at the same hotel were a family from the town I grew up in from the ages of ten to eighteen. I found this strangely comforting.

The parents were mid to late fifties and the four kids at a guess ranged from 16 to 24 years. Next to my chaos, their holiday seemed so relaxed and civilised. They sat by the pool drinking rose, their grown-up kids coming and going. Sometimes together sometimes alone. All very calm.

"One day, I am going to be just like you." I said to them as I passed their table one afternoon. Django on my hip, holding Cleo's hand, looking for Jim who was off on an exploration normally to the kitchen in search of ice cream and who knows where Brody's son was. He was twelve now, a fine boy, happy to do his own thing when the mood required. I just hoped he wasn't trapped in a wave or current in the sea or something. They looked at me and smiled. A chilled bottle of rose sat in between their books, magazines and newspaper.

I would make camp in the morning at one of the tables that went into the shade just after 12 pm so that there was some shelter for the chicks. Django was eight, nearly nine months old and showing strong signs of wanting to crawl. The other two had started walking at ten months. That would have catapulted the holiday into a different category where I'd be following him around whilst keeping tabs on the other two. So every time he got on his hands and knees, I scooped him up and popped him back on his bottom! Jim kept escaping to the kitchen where he had found lovely people to feed him ice cream. We had Lena with us once again. The routine was the same. I'd take over at breakfast then hand them back after bath time, ready for bed.

It was a lovely holiday and I was still convinced I could keep us together, making it as a family. **It nearly fell** apart one night though. It was Lena's day off and we had gone out to supper, all of us. Jim now three years old could sit at the table, Cleo still just about needed a highchair, and Django was in the front seat of the double buggy parked up at the table. Food started arriving. I went about dishing out bits and pieces onto plates for them and putting nibbles into Django's podgy little fists. Whilst I was leaning over to him, I knocked his bottle of milk over which rolled onto the floor. I whispered a 'bugger' under my breath which Brody must have heard.

"I faHkin knew ya wouldn' be able ta cope on ya own."
He laughed his sarcastic belly laugh. He was laughing **at** me.

"Here's the thing, I'm **not on my own**." I replied in a rare, heated flash of exasperation.

A little bit later, Brody's eldest son, at the heady heights of twelve, whispered in my ear, "Jennie, did Dad actually want to have children?" Bless him. He always helped when I asked him and although I was careful about the frequency, I often felt it was too much. But he always had a smile on his face.

"Well, they were all sort of planned, believe it or not," I replied. If I hadn't been so in love with them and being a mum, I definitely would have questioned my sanity. Other people clearly were questioning my sanity which came to light in later years.

The following night during and after dinner sitting at the pool bar, I got drunk. I would always have a decent amount to drink anyway. A couple of cold beers or rose during the day by the pool and a cocktail in the evenings followed by wine with dinner. That night, I went back on to the cocktails after dinner. We only had two nights left and I was feeling dread I think, about returning home or maybe I just felt like getting drunk. Brody was with me at the bar. I became a little bolshy in my attitude, the jaw came out. About what exactly I can't really remember. It could have been any number of things, his attitude to the hotel staff, spending some time with any one of the kids; anyway, he was responding as he only knew how.

"Yah faHkin drunk, Lee," he said. I vaguely remember predicting there was more verbal to follow so, I nailed my cocktail, stripped down to my knickers and dived into the lit pool. Momentary solace. Everyone was watching. Brody left.

One of the bar team was waiting for me with a couple of linen napkins and my pile of clothes. I patted myself down, then slipped my dress back on. They were very gracious as if this happened most nights! I wandered back to the room. I felt great. Was it a flash of defiance? I am not sure. There was a time when he would have loved me doing such a thing. Not anymore. He let me into our room to a simple,

'CuHnT', emphasis on the T.

Why couldn't he pronounce his 'T's' in regular conversation? The next day was our last. We all felt sad. It was strange because at home I wouldn't have to see him all day which was a big relief but on holiday, he was nicer because he had us doing exactly what he wanted us to do and providing for it. Big man. Big wallet. Pretty wife. Lots of children. It fed his ego.

We returned and life carried on in routine. Autumn arrived. It was beginning to dawn on me that the level of verbal abuse I was receiving was not normal or ok. A few remarks from my group of mums' were beginning to sprout further doubt, honestly as if I needed it, stirring what was already buried. I mentioned to one that I had to have the house tidy and toys away before Brody returned in the evenings/night.

"Or what?" She said looking at me in surprise.

"Or there's some sort of consequence," I said, "normally in some loud phrases such as FaHkin tidy this shit up." I mimicked him.

"Well, that would get one single reaction from me," she said simply, "middle finger up on both hands."

Oh, myyy godd…Other partners were different. Most even helped.

What was I really putting up with? The problem was that because I was trying to protect him all the time, I never opened up as to what went on in our house in terms of expectations of me, who said what and who was responsible for what. But once that little crack of insight was made, it soon grew into a gaping hole. Another moment happened when I was shopping at the big local supermarket. I had one of the big trolleys and in it, I sat all three children piling food around them. I bumped into one of the mums from the group. It was a Saturday morning.

"Wow!" She said. "You shop with all the kids?"

"Well, yes," I replied. "Where are yours?" She had two boys who were clearly not with her!

"With Stephen," (their dad!) she said looking at me with a kind of weird, surprised look.

He looked after the children? I too was soo surprised. He was a corporate man of the moment and I didn't think for one second that he'd even be around on a Saturday morning. The cascadein full flow.

I thought back to my own dad and my stepfather. Their pattern of fatherhood was all I knew really. I was the first in my peer group to have children so no comparable there. My upbringing firstly in Africa had been all about being at the expat clubs. Parents would play golf and then hang out at the bar whilst kids ran around from a very early age plus my father travelled frequently for work. Following that, my mother and stepfather had six children between them so we had a live-in au pair. I did think about both of them from time to time and reasoned to myself that the level of involvement from Brody somewhat reflected theirs. However, what I didn't factor in, was that situations were extremely different. When my parents divorced, my dad took holidays with us very seriously and took us places on his own, then later with my stepmum. They were always very together on holidays. In the early days, we would go back to our home in Africa where he would be the sole parent, he'd make it work. We would catch up, chat and go shopping altogether. My brother was three.

One evening, Brody came home early to have supper with me. The kids were all bathed and we were getting milk ready in the kitchen to go up for a story. I had got a few things out of the freezer for us which were defrosting on the side.

"Wass vat?" He asked coming into the kitchen and pointing at the defrosting food. I can't remember what it was now maybe fishcakes, I'm not sure.

"That's part of our supper. I thought I'd do beans and a salad too," I said.

"'FaHkin ell. I'm not eatin vat shiTe." He turned round to our three little children and said, "Ya muvva's a cuHnT." I went quiet, recognising a few signs. He'd had a long probably very nice lunch.

"What's a cunt, Daddy?" An inquisitive Jim. He always asked lots of questions and I loved him for it.

"A CuHnT is a faHkin CuHnt son," was Brody's answer.

With that, I picked up Django and shepherded Jim and Cleo upstairs with their milk. I had to address the fact that word couldn't be used whilst dressing down that their dad had called their mum it. We nestled into the bean bag in Jim and Cleo's room about to start a story then said, "I think Daddy is a bit disappointed in what I was going to prepare for supper and used a not-very-nice word. It's a word only for Daddy and I don't want to hear it again. Is that understood, you two?"

Obviously, Django couldn't talk yet. They nodded solemnly and with that, I started one of their books. A gigantic pang of hate lingered in my heart eating away at my adamant belief that we were all meant to be together. It was just a bit tricky because he was a bit different. I needed to steer the way to make it work. Provide the united front for us and re-plot his old course of betrayal to one of loyalty and to be unified as a family. I felt that was my job. I could not accept defeat, for him, for our children and especially not for me.

We plodded on.

Chapter 11
Is This It? My Life

Just before Django turned one, I decided it was high time to quit smoking. I managed quite easily with every pregnancy but one of the first things I did when I got home from the hospital was smoke a cigarette. Strange, huh? I didn't smoke often just when I had a drink and bearing in mind I wasn't allowed or rather Brody wouldn't have any drinking in the house unless we had guests; it was only on work days when I would finish the day with a glass of wine or when out with Brody and friends that I would have one. The problem was that when smoking, my wine consumption, escalated and I was increasingly unable to hit the stop switch when I was out. More like the self-destruct switch. I felt it was getting a little out of control and I needed to do something to address it. There was a hypnotist who had her practice round the corner from Oasis who used to come in sometimes. She had a lovely way about her plus her practice was growing. There had to be something in it. I asked her if she tackled smoking and she did. So I booked and went in for my appointment not knowing what to expect. When I walked in, I immediately felt relaxed. It was such a simple yet cozy atmosphere with a comfy couch, a coffee table overflowing with psychology magazines and her chair placed, probably strategically, to one side so as not to be in any way confrontational.

We started chatting about life and why I wanted to give up smoking. I explained my smoking status quo habit.

"Why can't you have a glass of wine at home?" She asked.

I explained that Brody's aunt used to drink quite a bit on her own and then to disguise it, used to decant wine into a teapot. She became a semi-functioning alcoholic and he was frightened that if we drank at home, especially me because I was home alone regularly, we would follow suit.

She appeared to appreciate that but went on to ask me other questions about home and if any other situations prompted me to want to have a cigarette. I outlined a moment just recently when we were having a family roast with the usual three veg, roast potatoes, peas and carrots. Brody liked his carrots cooked with a lot of sugar and I was beginning to find it quite sickly. I don't know why. I guess tastes change. I asked him if my carrots could be done without the sugary water. I was quite happy to do them myself. The response I got was, "Yoove 'ad sugar in ya carrots since I've known ya coz I've bin cookin' 'em like vat for ya. So yool continue havin' 'em like vat coz **I'm** doin' ve cookin', not yu." Thin lip.

I really wanted a cigarette but instead, I ate sugary carrots.

She looked at me. No pity, just understanding which was surprisingly comforting. But then she said, "And how do you cope, as in what is your coping mechanism when he talks to you like that?"

I started weeping. Bloody hell, what was wrong with me? I seemed to be shedding tears quite frequently at the drop of a hat.

"I don't have one," I answered feeling sad and pathetic. "I used to be able to just tell him to fuck off and turn it into banter but these days with kids and our setup, the consequences are just too unbearable."

"I understand," she came back with and then...

"I am going to build into the hypnotherapy a glass wall concept that you will carry around you and when he speaks to you like that, his words will ping off the glass wall and not enter your soul or psyche. Does that make sense to you? Can you visualise a glass wall surrounding you? A bit like an open-lidded jar with you inside."

I nodded. I was a little sceptical but I could see it. His words were discarded on the floor, lying there having no effect on me. That was going to be life-changing on a day to day basis for me.

She asked me to start breathing. Slowly. In through my nose, out through my nose. Then she asked if I was completely and utterly comfortable. I nestled down further into the sofa.

Her voice dropped a couple of octaves describing green fields, trees, blue skies and birds. Then I woke up. Forty-five minutes had passed by. I felt quite groggy as you do awakening from a deep sleep. She handed me a glass of water and waited patiently for me to get it together.

Oh god, was I supposed to fall asleep? Had I missed all the hypnosis?

"You may need a follow-up session, you may not. The only way you'll know is by being out there amongst smokers and facing your partner the next time he talks to you in a derogatory or demeaning way." She explained. "Just let me know."

And off I went. Back to Oasis where people were drinking and smoking. I walked in and I kid you not, the first whiff of cigarette smoke made me feel sick. Wow! Don't forget smoking was still allowed inside at this point in time, we were only just facing rumours of the ban which was probably going to be introduced soon which it did in the year 2007.

I went home feeling a little odd whilst pleasantly surprised. I didn't smoke for eighteen months. Brody's words struggled to get through my glass wall. The whole experience gave me what I can only describe as a bit of a new lease of life. ***I can do this,*** I genuinely thought. It was like having an epidural. A reprieve from the pain. Sadly though, that was temporary as was the hypnosis effect. Unlike an epidural which is there to get you through temporary pain, my pain was embedded in my everyday life, long term and no matter what I did, it showed absolutely no signs of easing.

Christmas was looming. I was head down organising Christmas parties at Oasis. We had a core group of uni students that came back for holidays and stepped back onto the rota which was a godsend as December was our best-ever busiest month of the year; a mixture of sports, Christmas and people looking for love. We catered for it all.

Family-wise, it was the first Christmas that the kids were properly understanding of the festive activities. Jim and Cleo had their first joint nativity performance at the nursery. It was magical. Jim was a reindeer and Cleo an angel. They were so sweet, so young. I sat on the benches at the back of the little hall, Django now one, on my lap, with the rest of the parents listening to their infant voices singing an eclectic mix of songs that we had practised at home. They knew that a fellow called

Santa was going to come down the chimney and leave pressies under the tree.

The wonderful questioning came with it all. 'How does he fit?'

'Should we clean the fireplace?'

'How do the reindeer **actually** fly, do they have wings?'

I remember my mother telling me that she saw him one Christmas. He had delivered presents and he was back on his way, in the sleigh and she had spotted it flying away. I explained that I had never seen him but she definitely had.

That Christmas was possibly the last whisper of any family happiness. The kids were one, two and three years old.

Christmas day, we were at my parents. My brother was back living in London and other family friends joined us all for a feast. My stepmother always did a superb spread with all the trimmings. I felt it was a happy day. Brody really liked my parents and thought they really liked him which meant he was always on reasonable behaviour in their company. Thank godddd.

Looking at us, through a window, you would have absolutely no idea of the angst only a layer down of my parents at having him in their house, seeing me with him and our three little children seemingly happy. They had no idea what went on behind the happy family scene. No idea of the denial I was in. We rarely saw them as a family. My dad would pop in and see me at Oasis. And I would take the kids over to see them when I could; when I had access to the car.

New Year's Eve that year we spent at Oasis. Lena babysat for us and we joined in the party with a handful of Brody's friends meeting us there. We had fun. No one had any idea of the true status quo.

Brody was busy working on our next little getaway. The Albatross Hotel in Cascais, Portugal. The first week of March. My parents were having Jim and Cleo and Lena moved in to look after Django. We had three nights and two full days. The 24 hours prior to our little trips were always a military operation for me; however, I felt it was all worth it as they were always a big treat. Brody spoilt me with the location, food and wine plus he had me exclusively to himself and was always on his best behaviour. This trip though kicked off with his disappointment in our room. It was a perfectly lovely double room overlooking the sea; however, he had thought he was getting us a suite. He wanted to deliver for me, and I completely understood, this was why I was always so touched by his efforts on these wonderful little breaks away. A lifeline for us as a couple. Once we were checked in and I was unpacking, he got on the phone with the travel agent who had organised it all.

"'It's a FaHkin mess Toby. I told ya I wan'ned a suite." He was shouting. I remember feeling very embarrassed for the poor guy. It was his first dealing with Brody and he probably didn't know what had hit him.

By this point in time in our life together as parents, I had figured out there was only one way to get out of the house when Brody would be ok to look after the kids and that was to go running. We had fitness as a common interest. I used to run a lot. I ran the London marathon the year before I met him plus exercise was 'allowed' as it kept me in shape. As a result, I was currently in pretty good shape. I suggested that we go for a run together on the beach. It was a beautiful afternoon and we ran along the sea edge where the sand was slightly wet which made it hard, easier to run on. We did some easy laps followed by sprints. By the time we had recovered, showered and had a couple of beers in our hands sitting in the bar overlooking the sea, he was in good spirits. We had a nice time. It was a shot of hopefulness for me as I was becoming tired. Tired of not knowing what to expect every day; of having to have tactics for every scenario, of starting every day without any emotional credit and tired of having to fend off irrational parenting.

On top of all of this, I had finally lost all strands of respect for him. That keyhole of awareness had grown into a magnified view of his true character, a slow but alarming awakening as to how he treated me, and made me feel inadequate, needy, useless. Sleeping with him was becoming increasingly uncomfortable but I didn't know what to do with all of this. I had to keep going. Isn't that what we are supposed to do for our family, the kids? Didn't most couples experience the same thing? I didn't know because I didn't ever open up and discuss with anyone else the nuances we had in our relationship. As far as anyone looking in could see, it appeared that I thought he was wonderful and he spoilt me.

The guilt started weighing in. It was my fault that I had given the kids such a father. I chose to have all three of them with him thinking I was creating a united front, a new togetherness/belonging for him and it was my failure that it hadn't panned out like the vision I had had. He must have had a vision too. He never wanted me to leave him. No one would love me like he loved me even in his funny old way. These flashes of vulnerability popped up frequently. A victim of his own family experiences and treatment. I was the one he had chosen to make it all better and I hadn't been able to. I was genuinely confused as to what I did to make him respond in the way that he did. Perhaps if I tried harder…

That summer was his 48th birthday so I decided to try and do something a little more special. He had a favourite green suede waistcoat which was becoming a little old-looking. I took the measurements of it and chose a deep burgundy-coloured leather and sent them off to a recommended tailor to be made into a replica; obviously in a different material and colour.

It arrived in time and looked really good. I organised all his favourite friends as a surprise to be at our favourite Chinese restaurant the one we went to for special occasions or as a treat.

The morning of his birthday, the kids and I gave him his present which he opened in the kitchen during breakfast. He oohed and aahed. He liked it! Then he tried it on. It was too small. Somehow the measurements had come up short.

"'It's too faHkin small. JESUS Cryyst." He half laughed half scoffed. My heart sank. One of his friends called his mobile phone. (yes he had his own phone by now) The friend must have asked if he'd got a present yet because we heard Brody shout down the phone.

'A useless faHkin leva waistcoat that don' fit.'

"I am sure the tailor can amend it," I said when he got off the phone feeling the whole thing had been a disaster. The kids looked on slightly confused at the early morning outbreak. They were currently one, three and four and could understand that Mummy had not delivered a very good present for Daddy. The evening surprise went down with the same anchor. Whilst Brody was pleased to see his friends, he ended up paying for the whole thing because he couldn't bear the difficult topic of the bill. I thought this was really strange as he ate out with this lot all the time. They must have discussed paying a bill on numerous occasions.

"Nice bu nex time, no surprises, please, Lee," he said in the taxi on the way home. "Not a grea'day, eh? Shit present and then I end up payin' for everyone to ave a top meyal."

Oh, myy godd, what had I done? I felt terrible. How could I not get a birthday right? I organised multiple events and meetings at Oasis all the time. It should have been a simple yet great birthday ending in hugs and kisses. I focused on our summer holiday. This year, we were off to Cyprus and one of 'our' closest friends was joining us for a week. Company. I was very pleased that he was coming; he was great with the kids and a happiness saver for me for Brody to have a mate which in turn took the pressure off. But he was only joining for the second week.

The first week was excruciating. For some reason, Jim was playing up, more than his usual cheeky self, he was behaving badly. He was four, about to start school after the summer holidays. Brody refused to parent him not recognising the behaviour. He called me a draconian whilst insisting they could have as many ice creams as they wanted. It was hot. It would cool them down. The kids obviously loved him for it. I was very frustrated. To escape just for a little bit, I went running every day at about 6 pm. I was fit because of all the running and with a splash of a tan, freckles out; I was looking really good.

"I fink you're avin an affair, Lee." He came out with, one night at dinner.

Oh, myy goddd. I actually started laughing. When did he think I would have the time? Not to mention that anyone would be so scared of him that they wouldnt touch me with a barge pole. I think he was feeling, whether he knew it or not that he was losing me. Or that he could lose me. His attitude towards me that first week was obscene. He berated me for doing a shit job at Oasis. Hiring useless 'CuHnts'. I wouldn't be able to do any other job. It was endless. I cried, literally with relief when our friend arrived. It made a difference and I was extremely grateful. On the plane going home, our seats were dispersed. There were three together at the front. Three dotted randomly down the rest of the plane. He sat himself, his mate and Jim in the three seats together. He put Cleo who was three years old in a seat next to random strangers in the middle, Lena five rows back then me with Django on my lap in the back row.

Oh, myyy goddd. It was a long flight going up and down checking on Cleo with Django on my hip who just wanted to be with his father.

One night, soon after we got back and school and nursery had pulled us back into routine, I was ironing downstairs. We had eaten supper in front of a favourite TV series and Brody had gone up to bed. Victoria texted me. There was a party going on just a few roads down from us. An Oasis regular was throwing his annual summer bash and I had missed the last two, possibly three. My initial reaction of course was absolutely not. I would have to go up and ask Brody if he didn't mind me going, to which he would of course mind. I couldn't bear having the conversation. It would be humiliating and unreasonable. I looked out the window and wondered who would be there. Most of the regulars from his crowd plus knowing him, he may have invited the whole place one night. It would be soo good to see them all in non-work mode.

I looked out the window. The window. It was open by about three inches and I could open it further, enough for me to climb out which meant the front door wouldn't alarm Brody. I could go for a couple of drinks and be back before he noticed. I decided to leave the iron on in case he came down and would think I was in the loo at the back of the kitchen. I texted Victoria to say I was on my way for one or two then I'd have to get back. I donned some lip gloss and eased the window up, climbed out and put it back in the position it was. Looking in, you would think I had nipped to the loo. I went. It was soo good to be out. I probably stayed double the amount of time I meant to. One conversation had a big impact on me. I was talking to one of our old team members, catching up.

"And how are **you?**" She asked after we had covered her news and my kid's news. "Still sleeping with the enemy?"

Dingalinggalingggggg. Oh, myyy goddd.

Yes, I was.

I had climbed out of a window of my own home to be there with my friends for a few drinks. What the hell was I doing living like this?

I realised though, that minute, that I needed to get home. I was skimming my chances of staying out so long and I had no idea what was waiting for me when I returned. I raced home and eased in through the window. The iron was off.

I put the ironing away, turned off the lights, took a deep breath and ventured up the stairs.

He was asleep.

Thank goddddddddddd. Thank you, God.

As quietly and softly as possible, I took off my clothes and slipped very carefully into bed. The consequences would come in the morning.

They did. A barrage of abuse although he was more angry at my leaving the iron on. I had my glass wall around me and the words sprung off. I was getting good at this. Practice. However, the more horrific ones did get through like when he said,

"Ya fahkin muvva's a CuHnt, ya sista's a CuHnt and you're a CuhHnt." This was after I had asked him not to let Jim, at the age of three and a half, watch 18-rated movies. The one in particular showed native American Indians being scalped and the scalps hung up on lines of rope. I had felt sick.

The school had asked us to come in to talk to the headmistress about some drawings Jim had done. They were of men and spears and lots of blood. He was four. She asked us specifically about it.

On our Thursday nights, we would often go to the theatre. Our town has this beautiful 800-seater theatre that opened in 1870. I loved these nights. The productions always put Brody in a good mood; he was always on time for them and we went out for a late supper afterwards. Because we were there so often, we decided to join as members and use the members' room which was sweet. We had our regular spot and it was table service. One night, it was the summer of 2005; Brody turned up after a very long lunch. In fact, he had come straight from the lunch. He got frustrated and a touch aggressive with the waitress because her English wasn't great and I'm not sure she had heard of Campari. The manager came over. He was extremely polite and Brody was not.

"Ya need to hire people who kin speak faHkin English."

The manager delivered the first warning which surprisingly he took and the manager served our drinks. The routine was we preordered interval or half time as Brody insisted on calling it and they would be waiting for us with complimentary crisps.

However, this night, they weren't. He was bristling and the poor girl was shaking after he shouted down to her from the other end of the room.

The manager came and delivered the last warning. The rest of the guests were looking at us with a mixture of disgust and angst awareness. Thank god, I didn't know any of them. I excused myself to go to the loo. On my way back...it crossed my mind that I had a choice as to go back in there or not. The thought of going back into that room was overwhelmingly horrendous. I made the decision not to. I knew it would have repercussions in the morning but I just couldn't bear it. I left, heading for Oasis. O, myy godd, how embarrassing. Why was there always an issue? Poor girl, I felt so sorry for her. I wondered if he would go to the second act. I thought I would just have a drink at Oasis, take a breath and head home.

Situations like these are so difficult in weighing up the consequences. I knew my decision to leave without him would bring the worst. However, I wasn't prepared for what actually happened. I had just taken a sip from a second drink bought by one of my favourite regulars when I happened to glance out the big curved window and down the road.

There, waiting to cross the road was Brody with all three sleepy children in their pyjamas, dressing gowns and Django's blanket, standing with the babysitter, who was looking completely bewildered.

The regular customer standing next to me saw my expression and followed my look, then he turned back to me with this sort of forlorn face without a minuscule of surprise and said, "I feel for you."

I grabbed my bag, said an extremely quick thanks and see ya and ran out of the door, across the road without looking and as gently as possible, took Django out of his arms. I asked the babysitter to grab Jim's little hand and I took Cleo's with my spare. I couldn't look at Brody. I wanted to scream at him, hit him, smack that big round smug face with all my might but instead, I asked her how they got there and she explained the car was right around the corner.

"Come on, chickens," I said, "last bit of the midnight adventure."

I heard Brody behind me saying in a loud voice, "Your place is wif me and the children. Who dya fink you are? Ya supposed to be a FahHkin Muvva." Then he walked into Oasis and sat at the bar to order a drink where he stayed until closing before coming home. Why had I left? I knew there were going to be consequences but I didn't think for one minute that he'd physically involve the children.

I got them home and re-tucked them up with surprisingly little queries. I think they were still sort of in a sleepy, trustful trance. I thanked and apologised to the babysitter who looked at me with that pity I had become used to. She also worked at Oasis so whoever didn't see this little trick of Brody's was certainly going to hear about it. More pity.

The next morning was as usual. No mention of anything; in fact, just silence towards me and chit-chat about the day ahead at school with the children. I simply kicked into routine.

This is what my life had become. A series of awful events, getting through them and then pretending it was all ok.

I was exhausted.

Chapter 12
Murder

Not long after the theatre night incident, I was working a Friday night. This wasn't a hugely regular occurrence. I tended to work the Friday daytime whilst the kids were in nursery and either be home to do supper or on the odd occasion, I would ask my helper to bring them to Oasis and we'd have supper there, together. One of our regulars had started a blind dating concept where he would arrange four potential matches for each of the ladies strategically positioned in bars around town and the men would have half an hour visiting each chosen four. We were one of the venues plus provided the venue for the after-party, exercising our late-night licence—we had to have food to serve. They were fun, busy nights; however, I thought it was important that whilst in our late licence zone, that we have the licensee on site. I was that person.

So once a month, I worked it. On those nights, I had our lovely helper take over at six, bath and put the kids to bed. Brody promised that he would be home by nine or ten latest so she could go out or home, as well as to keep childcare costs down. This one particular Friday, we had our favourite musician in the house. He had been playing live music, on his guitar at Oasis for years and years. Pre-me! He was part of the furniture. So he played a few sets and then a little bit for the after-party with the dating lot. I was very aware of noise and activity as we had been getting some grief from a new neighbour who kept brandishing the fact that his wife was a barrister. I pointed out that we had been there way before them and that if she was that smart perhaps her due diligence and research could have been a bit sharper or their joint decision to move next to a bar that had live music playing weekly for nearly eight years, but that just infuriated him even more. Dickhead.

Anyway, this particular night, we cleared everyone out by 1 am, cleaned up by 1.30 am and then had a drink with Ricardo, the musician who incidentally lived just past me and had offered to stay and walk me home. Lovely. We must have left just after 2.15 am so it was past two thirty that Ricardo said goodbye at the end of my road to carry on to his home. Maybe nudging about an hour later than I usually reached our house. I turned my key in the lock as quietly as possible and stepped inside. I had just closed the door and was taking off my shoes sitting on the bottom step when I heard a flurry of movement with heavy breathing coming down the stairs behind me. Before I could turn around, I felt Brody's steel grip in the thick of my hair at the top of my head followed by a sharp stinging pain over the top of my scalp as he dragged me up the stairs. I tried to use my feet on the steps to lift my body up to try and alleviate the pain whilst using one hand to dig my nails into his wrist and the other to un-prise his fingers. He was, of course, far too strong.

"Where the faHk 'ave you been, you cuNting whore. Ya been aert shagging." It was a statement.

My protests were absolutely pointless. Dragging me past the kids' bedrooms into ours, he threw me on our bed and ripped the zip open on the black chords I was wearing. He pulled them down to my knees with just a fraction of his strength whilst telling me he was going to…

"Check ya cunt for sperm." which he did by shoving two fingers up inside me. I'm guessing he didn't find what he was looking for as he grunted sort of in dismay, removed his fingers which he then sniffed, climbed into bed and rolled over with a final 'cuNt'

I was in complete and utter shock. My scalp throbbed and I felt disgusting having had his two fingers grappling around up inside me. I did not know what the fuck to do. I sat up and took a couple of deep breaths. What was clear was that whatever I did next had to disturb him the very least if at all. If I left the room, I knew he would come after me. I wouldn't be able to get to the front door quick enough because I'd need to pass his side of the bed plus that would mean leaving the kids inside. That was categorically not an option. There was only one thing for me to do. I slowly and very quietly took off my trousers which were now down around by my ankles and the rest of my clothes and with the least bit of movement possible, inched the duvet over me and lay there wide awake. For hours. No tears. Just shock, followed by pure, white, hatred.

I must have finally drifted off because the kids woke me in the morning. I did what I always did.

Our daily routine started with the alarm going on weekdays or kids jumping into bed on weekends. I would get

Django out of his cot to waddle into our room whilst I went downstairs to prepare morning milk for the children and tea for us along with a selection of Brody's vitamins and supplements which included a cod liver oil capsule. That morning, still in a state of disbelief whilst I was preparing drinks and pills, I looked at the large oily capsule and wondered how possible it would be to inject some form of poison into it.

How much could I fit into the capsule? Would the oil ooze out be alerting that it wasn't quite right? This train of thought took all about ten seconds when I broke the reverie as the tray was complete and I went back upstairs to distribute tea, tablets and milk. Every morning from then for roughly a week, I would take the theme one step further, initially just enjoying the image of a very sick then dead Brody leaving me and the kids in peace to live our lives.

Which poison?

How much would it take to make an effect on his enormous physique?

Where would I store it? The syringe and bottle would have to be kept separately. Where would I buy it? It could just be rat poison. A hardware store…

What if he went to the doctor feeling ill and they took tests?

What if he found it or the syringe? Poison, I could possibly explain away or even pre-empt that perhaps I had seen a rat? We had found a dead one recently in Oasis so it wasn't completely off the radar. The syringe with a needle though …

What if when he died, they did a post-mortem?

What if the cause of death was actually figured out and I went to prison? The children...I wouldn't see them every day, cuddle them, tuck them up. They would see me in prison.

WHAT the FUCK was I thinking? Jesus. And there it was, my light bulb moment.

I had to get a grip. The realisation that my situation was so bad, desperate and I had to leave, started sinking in rapidly like a version of the Titanic. Big and very real. I was genuinely thinking about how to murder him. This was not even vaguely rational from whatever angle you looked at it.

The weight of this realisation was heavy and grew heavier throughout the day as I processed reality and shed any wisps that were left of the facade leading to what lay ahead which was overwhelming like being winded and unable to gasp in air. How do you approach a conversation, and kickstart the steps to leaving a man like Brody? I felt, colossal dread and fear and immediately drained. I kept those ripped chords at the bottom of my wardrobe to remind me every day. Stay strong. Get out.

The next few days were tough. I plastered on a smile and attempted to tackle every day as if everything was normal. The most important thing was to remain the same whilst I made a plan which included all sorts of factors, the children, their emotions, feelings and questions. Their school and routine. Where to go? Money. If I didn't manage to stay consistent and Brody sensed something was up, I wasn't sure how he would behave towards me and the children. I had to tread very carefully; however, I did take the tiniest bit of solace knowing that despite what was to come, on the other side, waiting for me was some sort of freedom. **I just had to get there.** Believe that I could.

The other factor was that no one except for Victoria possibly, knew the true scenario. I knew she had a strong inkling because we were together a lot and he was always around as well as the fact that on a couple of occasions, I had burst into tears on her shoulder. But we had never discussed it openly. At the end of the day, we were colleagues and I had to keep a professional line regardless of how well we got on. But now I broke down once more, my head on her shoulder in the office at work the Monday after having endured two days with Brody at home over the weekend. Finally. I cried and cried. I didn't talk. She didn't need an explanation. She just let me sob away. She asked me one question though,

"Can I do anything?" To which I sadly shook my head. The only person who could do anything was me. Only me.

As for everyone else, the happy facade I had built and surrounded us with, out of pure pride, was believable. I had no one else to talk to.

Oasis was at this point up for sale and the shareholders had pledged me a small lump sum upon receipt of funds in appreciation for the work I had put into growing the business over the years. I wasn't sure quite how much but I knew it wouldn't be an insult and guessed that it would be roughly three months' salary. Enough to get us out. After that, I would beg, borrow even steal to keep things ticking and surely he would provide me financially to cover a few basic things, clothes, clubs and school lunches. He had provided for his eldest and always reiterated it was for him to have a life where he didn't go without. Surely, he would feel the same about Jim, Cleo and Django?

The first person I confided in was my stepmother. I had come to realise that she and my dad had not one tinyy-weeny iota of like for Brody. When exactly that penny had dropped in my mind, I am not quite sure. Possibly just over time, the lack of invites, interest and general contact. The kids had a minimal yet lovely relationship with them for which I was exceedingly grateful. So, one day she was dropping me home from an infrequent solo visit to their house, something to do with health and wills. My dad's health had been riddled with various operations and they were just getting their ducks in a row. They had wanted to see us all although my sister still being in Australia, it was just my brother and I. Anyway, after all the discussions which I tried desperately not to find morbid, she offered me a lift home. In the car, I grabbed the moment, and it came out.

"I have to leave Brody," I said. "It has become unbearable."

"Oh, thank god," she said immediately, then quickly turned to look at me, "Are you ok, as in safe?"

Ohhhhhhhhhhhh, myy godd. The relief. I had told her the truth. Someone knew.

I felt like dissolving into tears as respite became a possibility with this first step, though I managed to dig deep and hold it together as we were ten minutes away from home, the children and very possibly Brody, who would be moody because I had been somewhere on my own. I needed my mask on.

I reassured my stepmum that at the moment, I was 'ok' although pleaded with her to keep this news to herself and Dad and just be aware that a plan was bubbling but it wasn't going to happen overnight. It transpired that they had been waiting patiently for this news for a very long time. She gave me a big, like never before hug. I got out of the car.

Chapter 13
The Plan

The plan was to introduce the idea of getting help without actually calling it 'help' to keep a positive tone on the whole thing. I had to feed his need to be in control of me otherwise the bad things happened. I had little idea of what was in store. I often wonder, looking back that if I had known, would I have done things differently? I am not sure I had too many options. It wasn't a case of packing up the kids and going somewhere. Where would I go with three little ones? The situation at home wouldn't have been deemed unsafe right then by any social care and if I turned up at someone's house with the three kids and a suitcase, answering questions on the status quo—I would look dramatic as the façade had been incredibly convincing. I had to live through it.

A marriage counsellor or rather relationship counsellor had to be the first step. Brody must be feeling that all was not well. His frustrations couldn't feel normal to him surely. I took the angle that if we could talk things out we would have a chance to get back to how things were, our 'united front' He knew that Oasis was up for sale and that it was possible a new owner wouldn't need me and I would be completely dependent on him which would play straight into the hands of his need for control and dominance. What he didn't know was that a small lump sum was coming my way. So, I hoped that the mixture of talking it out with someone to reignite 'us' and the increased dependency on him might sell it to him.

I carefully picked my moment to raise the topic. I was petrified. He had to be sober and feeling superior otherwise his insecurity traits would flare.

So, the moment when I had fed and bathed the kids then put them to bed, he had finished work, rowed and was about to shower to go out (without me) was the time I chose.

He was filling in his exercise diary which he did after every exercise session with great care as well as overlining each letter (not sure why, just a habit) he had had a good day work-wise and he was about to go out with one of his favourite 'clients', an old friend. I sat on the floor by his desk next to the rower and said.

"Have you got five minutes? I don't want to make you late, but I have an idea that I'm really hoping you'll think about." O, godd. Deep breath. I felt sick.

"Yes darlin', what is it?"

"What would you say if I asked you to come with me to talk to a Relate person to chat and explore where we are? I know I am frustrating you. What do you think? I just feel that we need to do a little exploring, do you know what I mean?" I had to stop myself from nervous rambling.

"Yes, of, course, darlin', let's talk about it tomorrow. I need to shower and leave in 30 minutes. Woodjya call me a cab?"

Phewwwwww. I breathed a large, silent sigh of relief. For now.

The next morning it wasn't mentioned nor the next. I was thinking about when to pick up the thread and get to the next stage when, on the third day, he came home and said he had been in contact with Relate. He was going in to have a session on his own next Thursday before our night out, to become familiar with what happens there. Bloody hell. Not surprising. He had taken control.

That Thursday finally came around. Each day felt like two days. The topic wasn't touched on at all. It felt as if he had taken ownership of the situation, and it was now his thing and his terms. I clung to the fact that regardless, I had made the first step, the first big step to freedom.

I met him at one of his favourite pubs in town. I had absolutely no idea what I was going to find. It could have anything from highly critical, negative scepticism to acceptance of the situation, maybe even his own lightbulb moment. I walked through the big heavy wooden door of the pub where I found him finishing off writing a card. A pint of Guiness in front of him on the table. The pub was busy, a decent hum provided the privacy I needed. He would not have cared about that.

"Get yaself a drink, Lee," he said, reverting to our affectionate old habit of calling each other by our surnames. He handed me a twenty.

When I got back to the table, he gave me the written card, in its envelope with a small flourish and said, "I've bin on vis incre'ible jurney tonigh'. We're gunna enter a new chapter in our lifes, and everyfin will be fine."

Jesus. Just like that. One solo session with a Relate Counsellor. Sorted. It took all my control to stay calm, reign in my frustration, indignation and ask about the session. Fucking hell.

The card was loud and colourful and in it were lines and lines of his handwriting all in capital letters explaining that he recognised we needed a fresh start. He loved me and our children. We had a top family; I was a top bird and he would be willing to make a bit more of an effort.

No one would love me as much as he did.

This was going to be excruciating. More so than what I had thought? I am not sure I had known what to expect. My frustration led to pity.

"She wonts ya to come for a session togeva," he said. Well, at least he was willing to give more time.

So, we went. A couple of times. She was lovely. She took us back to when we fell in love and beyond. The first stumbling block arose when we were going through pregnancies and she asked if I had had any others. Why and what relevance this had, I do not know but my first instinct was to be open and truthful. In fact, I had two aborted pregnancies; one when I was a young teenager and one just before Brody took me to our first date to the Thai restaurant. I had fallen pregnant with the rugger boyfriend I had been with at the time. I had not told Brody about this pregnancy because the chap was still around, he lived in our town and it was just as much his news as it was mine. So I had only told him about the teenage one. I forgot I had kept this from him; it was, after all over eight years ago and so much had happened since. I told the truth. He went ballistic. This was a good and bad thing. It was good because the counsellor saw him in action. Bad because it came home with us. Three days of silent treatment.

We went back. He complained that I was a shit cuNt mother working all the time. I ignored him. And that I was an alcoholic. She looked at me and asked me to hold out my hands. Which I did. "Brody," she said, "Jennie may drink too much in your opinion but I strongly believe she is not an alcoholic; she would be shaking and she would also be less lucid and articulate."

At the end of the second session, she asked to see me on my own. We were in the run-up to Christmas and she wanted to see me beforehand.

I went. Her message to me was crystal clear. She told me that she feared for my safety and I needed to get out of the house as soon as possible and could I do that? I explained that our visits were part of a process; that moving out was the very aim. I had to manage it carefully. We decided to schedule a joint session for the first week of January so that Brody was still under the impression that we were working on our relationship. She gave me an emergency number. Brody met me immediately afterwards—these were all on Thursday evenings as I had the sitter prebooked from 6 pm, and of course, he wanted to know what she had said and why the solo session…I focused on the drinking.

Christmas was tough. None of my family was around and there was no one to hook up with and nowhere to go for Christmas day; it was just us. I had a very late night the day before Christmas Eve with the Oasis team staying late for some Christmas drinks which meant I was extremely tired after only a few hours of sleep. A bit stupid really. I knew it would antagonise Brody. I spent the day of Christmas Eve wrapping pressies and shopping for our Christmas lunch the next day. I didn't lay the table.

We had decided to get the kids bikes that year. Jim was four, Cleo three and Django was two.

On Christmas day, we opened up our pressies amid a frenzy of wrapping paper. The kids obviously thought their new bikes had come from Santa. There was lots of excitement, smiles and laughter. Then we all went to the pub. The turkey was in. The table yet to be laid.

Whilst we were at the pub, outside only as kids weren't allowed in, Brody was on his fourth pint, his hand somehow rested on my bottom, and he gave it a good squeeze. I visibly flinched and moved away. It was an automatic reaction.

O myyy goddd.

"You faHkin bitch cuNt. I've 'ad enuf of ya. FaHkin out drinkin' with that useless faHkin lot. Ya supposed to be a wife and muvva. It's Christmas and faHkin table ain't even laid."

His lips were in that flat line position and I knew it was bad. We walked back and every window we could see into seemed to have a bloody beautifully laid table and he pointed out every one of them. It was like a constant slap in the face, especially when he pointed them out to the kids. The insinuation that I was useless.

We got in and he slammed his fist on the breakfast bar and shouted, "This is a faHkin joke. I'm not hangin aroun 'ere. Jim, come on, we're off." As he picked up the car keys. I pleaded for him not to go. Not to drive with Jim in the car. I would set the table; it wouldn't take me long, blah blah blah I felt pathetic. All I really wanted to say to him was FUCK OFF—you can help lay the table. Where was that united front you won me over with, you fucking wanker bastard? But I knew he would take off with Jim. Which he did anyway. For the whole day. Not answering his phone. I had no idea where they were or if anything had happened. He had been four pints down and I suspected that they would stop in a pub. Literally, all I could do was desperately hope they came home safe. I had to keep believing that soon we would be out of this hell of a way of life. I was so tired and ached for non-confrontational, happy surroundings.

At about 4 pm, I made the decision to eat turkey and trimmings with Cleo and Django. It was their Christmas too. We pulled crackers and put on hats and sat around the breakfast bar. I would suffer the consequences for not waiting. Just before 8 pm, they came through the door. Thank God. Thank you, thank you. I wrapped up Jim in a tight hug. He seemed fine; they had been to some woods, who knows where hunting the enemy. I felt exhausted with relief that they were home. I couldn't bear to look at Brody. I wanted to scream and shout and slap that big, round, head holding a fat smug look. Allowing myself a little gratification, I remembered the night when I was pregnant with Django driving to KFC when I planted the heel of my shoe into his face. Deep breath. That had felt so goddamn good.

I went about getting Jim fed and off to bed with Cleo and read a long story which I kept reading way past their little faces became blissfully relaxed that comes with that deep sleep. I then went straight to bed. Maybe a new day would reset the mood plus Brody had a Boxing Day rugby match to go to. The kids and I would be on our own, thank god. I messaged Victoria.

I asked her to meet me and the kids for a coffee in the morning. She actually lived just round the corner in between us was our favourite deli cafe. We met there. I delivered the news she had been expecting. It was a bit weird as I had to be cryptic so the kids didn't understand. I also had to hold back the tears. She took my hand and held it very tightly nodding her head. It didn't need too much explanation but I needed her help to look at accommodation for me and the kids. I didn't think about much in terms of agreements and separation details; I just knew I needed to get myself and the kids out of there. Plus, I needed a point of contact for the agent in case Brody cottoned on to the plan. Faced with the realisation that we were actually moving out, his reaction was likely to be volatile and for the first time, I felt some fear.

The first apartment we saw, Victoria came with me, we squeezed in first thing after the kids were dropped off and before work. We traipsed up two flights of black fire exit stairs outside the building before going into a lovely, spacious two-bed flat. I was desperate for it to be suitable. Victoria pointed out that every time I was with Django, I'd need to carry the buggy up and down. It just wouldn't work. The next one we saw was a small terraced house with a really cool, safe enclosed garden. It was just too much money for me though and they wouldn't budge on price. I was soo tempted but again Victoria pointed out that having a monthly financial struggle was the last thing I needed. I was assuming that Brody was not going to help financially for the kids. I was absolutely correct to assume that of course.

The third flat I saw on my own. The agent showed me to an upstairs duplex. It was sweet. Freshly painted open kitchen, living area in a happy yellow. It had two bedrooms, a modern bathroom and a wee bit of shared outside lawn space plus it was a very short walk to school. Perfect.

"This is it," I blubbed to the agent. We were in the main bedroom which was big enough for three little beds.

"Are you ok?" She said. She knew a little about my circumstances. The bare minimum as I had to explain it was just myself and the kids moving.

"Yes," I said, "it is pure relief." I explained.

"It is free in four weeks," she replied. Four whole weeks. Four weeks. The start of February.

Oh, myyy goddddddd. It felt like a lifetime yet tangible. I could feel us there. Freedom.

"I'll take it."

It transpired that the family who owned it were moving to America with the husband's job. They had a littl'un. I met with the lady as she was a tiny bit concerned about how three children would work. Over a coffee in the open-plan kitchen, I explained my situation and she listened. She put her hand on mine and said,

"You will be happy here, this is a happy place and I wish you all the best. You are doing the right thing." I fought back the tears.

So, the big fat thing was, how was I going to break it to Brody? And my blissfully ignorant children.

Meanwhile, at Oasis, the shareholders had found a buyer. I wasn't sad. It was time. I had been there for eight years. Victoria six. It was becoming increasingly difficult for me to concentrate on the business and be the mum I wanted to be. Nights were impossible, especially without the financial support from Brody. It had run its amazing course plus it couldn't grow anymore. Profit was as healthy as I could get it.

The shareholders had quietly watched my life from close by. They knew but didn't get involved. I knew they would be there for me if I needed however, up until this point, I had had something to prove and my pride to keep intact. I was involved in the due diligence part of the process as I knew the place inside out. They were giving me £5,000 as a thank you. Appreciation of the vision that increased business and profits. Brody, who now had wind of this plan expected half of it to go to him.

I broke the news a week later. So three weeks to go. I don't think he was actually that surprised. I positioned it that we needed a breather. Maybe for six months. Then take stock of how we felt. I would just take the bare minimum of stuff. I didn't think for one minute he would never give me the belongings I left behind. He never did. Some treasured things of my mum's, my own and my siblings. My brother eventually got his trunk from the attic though. Brody had always had a soft spot for him.

It was that night I floated the idea of sleeping in the spare bed. He couldn't bear it. I was tucked up with my nightie on, just drifting off when he came up into the loft room and turned on all the lights.

"I don wan ya faHkin up 'ere. Fahkin stu' pit. In my 'ouse you sleep wif me." I agreed to come back to bed but I wanted to keep my nightie on. He waited until I got into our room and then told me to take it off.

"No," I said, "I am keeping it on. What don't you get? I don't want to sleep naked next to you anymore. Don't you get it? I am moving out. We are having a break because I need space away from you."

"In my 'ouse, you do wha I wanya ta do." I didn't have a chance to remind him that technically it was my house because he had grabbed the material at the front of my neck, yanking it down so the buttons popped then he ripped it off.

"Now ge in ve bed, cuHnt."

"No." But with that last bit of defiance in me, he came right up to my face shouting.

"Get out ven. Get out my 'ouse." I slipped around him. He turned and chased me down the stairs which is where I found myself on all fours on the Welcome mat in the prologue. He had been right behind me and blocked the right turn at the bottom of the stairs leaving just a few metres to the front door for me to go. I stumbled to it and tried to block the latch with my body. He very nearly managed to get his hand on the doorknob and was about to open it when I sank to my knees begging and apologising.

The next day, the agent called to tell me the flat owner's departure had been delayed by a month. Moving in day was 1 March. This news brought on a panic attack. I had never had one before. It started with a major increase in my heart rate followed by shortness of breath then, I couldn't breathe.

Oh, myyy GOD. Whyyyyyyyyyyyyy?

I was at work and Victoria saw my state. She took my hand and sat me down. Minute by minute, I kept repeating to myself in my head, like one of those beat monitors that help you keep in time when you're playing an instrument. It was the only way I could do it. Some minutes went faster than others. Some minutes I would forget then remember. Thankfully, Brody seemed to be out most of the time. I avoided the house when I thought he would be home showering for client meetings.

Telling him I was there for another month was torturous. 'Ya faHkin lucky I still love ya Lee.' He said, looking at me with a self righteous, self satisfied look. Thin lipped.

The news started getting around amongst our close circle. I had updated my parents and told my very thankful siblings and close friends. Their jubilation motivated me to keep feeling the freedom. Tick tock.

My brother had his 30th birthday bash in a swanky London restaurant in early February. My sister had flown over for it, staying with my parents for a week. We sat quietly at the bar before everyone arrived.

"How are you?" She said simply.

"It has nearly broken me," I replied taking a big slug of wine. "But I'm going to make it. 19 days to go."

I almost expected him to blunder into the restaurant. He had been apoplectic that I wasn't taking him. I am not kidding.

One of the wives of Brody's close friends called me after she heard.

"Are you safe?" She had asked. I told her that I wasn't sure. I was frightened. But what could she do? What would I do now if someone said that to me? I have thought about this often my conclusion being that I would meet them as soon as possible. I would listen and if necessary take them and their children somewhere safe. My place or somewhere else. Because it just takes one tiny little moment to move from potential to actual.

A couple of nights later, Brody picked up Django and threw him at me. From roughly four feet away. I can't remember why. He wasn't crying, I think he simply wanted his mumma. We were both fine but what if I'd fallen, hit my head? Or I didn't catch him and he smashed into the wall? Both of which were possible. The repercussions of either were not bearable to think about. I had a week to go. Brody couldn't cope with the loss of control over me. It was as if he wanted to hurt me before it was too late. Tick tock. Beats per minute.

I left packing right until the last minute. Two days to go. As a result, I left quite a few things behind. It didn't matter so much about the kids' clothes as they would be coming back. This also placated Brody who was suddenly taking an interest in when he was going to see them. We had an extraordinarily calm conversation about a routine. He wanted at least one weekend day but two nights in a row. We settled on Sundays. I would drop them off after any sports like rugby and then they would spend two nights which meant he would drop off and pick them up after school on a Monday.

Oh, myyy goddd; I wouldn't see my kids for two nights. Big deep breath.

I honestly thought that he wouldn't care too much. Why? I am not sure as I had witnessed the fight with his ex-wife to keep his son in the country and he had had a strict routine agreed with her. I guess he had just seemed so fixated on his own schedule rather than ours as a family that it didn't occur to me that perhaps threatened with not seeing them, he would step up. And he did.

Chapter 14
The First Night: Pizza, Wine, Fags and Freedom

I carried out the flat inventory with the agent and got the keys the day before. I couldn't quite believe it. One more night. I suppressed the wander of thought as to what might lie ahead and switched to minute by minute mode. I picked the kids up from school and took them around to see the flat. It was our little adventure, I said. They were going to have bunkbeds and all be in the same room. The flat was a small walk from school where Jim was in Reception and Cleo was in Nursery, our local area that they knew and felt familiar with. They were so young that it didn't even dawn on them that their mummy and daddy were splitting up. Yet. That did come later though. I was literally just focusing on the first night.

We planned where the beds would go so that I could have it all set up when they got back from school the next day and that we would have pizza, coke and watch a movie on a school night! When we got back to the house for the last night, they were quite excited. Brody's radar was alerted. Why were they?

Why was he home?

That night he fell asleep with me in a tight hold. Naked of course. I almost didn't care. My boxes were packed. This was it. Tick tock. I drifted off. My heart rate was normal.

One of my great friends Sam who I'd met in Oasis had a big hatchback car and he had offered to help me move. Brody liked Sam which meant there would be no issues letting him in the house. Actually, it turned out that Brody left in the morning straight after saying goodbye to the children as we went off to school, ignoring me completely, understandably, and he stayed away the entire day. We did three car load runs. With the last load all packed up, I closed the door and posted my key through the letter box. I heard it drop onto the Welcome mat with the tiniest thud.

OHMY goddddddddddddddddddddddddddddddd.

I looked at Sam. I must have had a funny look on my face. I didn't know whether to laugh or cry, like when you hit your funny bone. He gave me a big hug and to keep the momentum said, "Come on, Jennie, in the car." And with that, we were off, back to the little flat so I could start making it a home.

I was eternally grateful to him. He's one of life's good'uns.

The beds did indeed arrive, Lena and I put them together. One bunk bed and one little, tiny bed for a two-year-old. Django was pottering about helping to 'unpack' and then before I knew it, it was time for school pick up. Lena left to go home; Django and I to school. Lena looked at me and in her strong Bolivian accent she said, "Theeze very good, Yennie." She ruffled Django's hair before going off to get her train home. She knew that our time together was coming to an end. I wasn't working which meant I had no income but also I didn't need help looking after the children. I was looking forward to having a stint at being a full-time mum although the clock was ticking on the small funds I had from the sale of Oasis. I needed to start looking for my next work venture very soon but right now I was focused on our first night and settling the kids.

At school, we picked up Cleo first from the nursery. There was a five-minute staggered pick-up time which was enough to cross the playground to the reception area to collect Jim. She was all smiles and keen to get out. Mrs Abbott who walked out with her, which was a bit weird, unusual, was also smiling. She whispered in my ear, "A little bird told me you're moving today. You're leaving the aRRse Hole?" She drew back a little to look at me. I was nodding in wonder. She squeezed my arm and very quietly said, "Well done."

"Thank you." I whispered, gathering up Cleo, putting her artwork under the buggy. I am not sure what I was expecting. I hadn't really thought about people outside of close friends having a reaction. Nobody had ever let on what they thought of him before, out of respect I guess or possibly that I had put up such a facade that no one knew the ugly truth, about how I actually felt. I'm not sure; it gave me a sliver of reassurance. Mrs Abbott had been the head teacher for eighteen years prior to taking on the nursery. She must have seen and experienced all sorts. She was a professional and one never really knew exactly what she thought despite her forthright approach. When Cleo started Reception class, six months later, she organised two bags of new sets of uniforms for us and hit the nail on the head when she said, "I'm assuming the arsehole isn't contributing."

Back to the moment, Jim was keen to get out of class that day too. Jumping about shouting 'bunk beds' he had bagsied the top bunk. Clearly a very exciting prospect. I was very thankful for distraction from not sleeping in the home they knew.

On the way home, we went via the Tesco local. We bought popcorn, coke, ice cream, wine and cigarettes.

They ran up the stairs to their new shared bedroom. Django who still couldn't talk bar his one word 'Well' was pointing to his unpacking and his little bed with Thomas the Tank Engine duvet cover.

"Well, well, well!" he said.

We ordered lots of pizza. We settled in on the three chairs I had managed to take that fit in Sam's car. One big comfy armchair that Django and I fitted in, snuggled together, and the two leather recliners, one each for Jim and Cleo. We chose a movie from a small selection of DVDs.

Whilst we were tucking into the popcorn, the first question came.

'When is daddy coming mumma?' Cleo's innocent little voice questioned.

Mmmmmmmmm. I hadn't thought of that one. Carefully I said, "He is going to let us enjoy the adventure first, especially, the first night, then come." That seemed to do the trick for that moment.

Brody had been adamant that he didn't want to know where we were going. The address of the flat. I had been absolutely fine with that. I didn't even find it strange that he didn't want to know where his children were. I guess he knew where they would be at school every day plus, he was expecting them on Sunday as we had agreed. I didn't want to think about that just yet. I had managed to move to hour by hour which felt like a holiday compared to minute by minute. The pizza arrived. More excitement. I opened my bottle of wine, poured myself a generous glass and we watched the rest of the movie eating and drinking all our treats.

The kids went to bed quite exhausted. We laid out their uniforms ready for the next day; Django chose what he was going to wear too. They claimed spots for their toothbrushes in the bathroom and climbed into their new beds tired and full. After a lengthy tuck-in with a story, I turned off the light closed the door and went downstairs.

I was utterly drained, jubilant yet completely sapped of any energy mentally and physically yet I couldn't give up relishing the new-found taste of freedom. Complete independence. I refilled my glass, smoked a cigarette on the doorstep and then sat on one of the recliners looking out to the sky peacefully watching as the night closed in. I could actually breathe. Just breathe. Finally, I climbed the small set of stairs, passed the silent kids room and into mine where I fell asleep completely exhausted on my own, in a nightie and free.

Epilogue

I found love surprisingly quickly. I had expected to be alone for quite some time having been told that no one would love me. Remember I had been told on a near-daily basis that no one would be interested in a cuNt like me. Damaged goods. And it had a decent dose of the desired effect. Only, someone who had been on my proverbial doorstep all along felt differently. One of my brother's closest friends from university. Kind, fun and very loving. Three months later, Brody broke into the little rental flat when I refused to answer his repeated telephone calls. He found us sound asleep in each others arms and I woke up to the crack of his fist hitting my new love's face. Then came the police, an ambulance and a whole other story. We made it though. Now eighteen years later, we are very happily married with one more chicken to add to the brood.

So there, you have it. My escape story. I would go through it all again, every minute knowing that I would be where I am today with the true, unconditional love of my husband, the relationship we have together and with the four children, three of them now young adults exploring their own relationships with the people in their lives …and with each other.

Authours Thoughts

I have come across as well as heard about many people, men and women making their partner's life a misery in order to somehow make themselves feel better or bigger. Feeding their insecurity. Like Brody. Clearly, these people don't recognise the trait. I heard just whilst writing this, of a friend from the distant past who nearly died in childbirth. She confided that life is so unbearable with her husband's mental abuse that she often wished in her darkest moments that she had. Sadly, the abuse has reduced her to such a lesser version of herself that I doubt that she will ever have the strength to leave him. Desperate and oh, so long.

I know of another couple, man and wife with three grown-up children where she made his life a misery for a very long time, many years, by constantly putting him down and antagonising him to get a reaction. Finally, he left for another lady. The ex-wife turned the children on him. They had been so close with their dad. It was brutal for him.

When miserable partners leave, they often use their children or money to prevent the other from experiencing any freedom or happiness. Why do they do that? **Everyone** becomes the loser, suffers. Damaged. And the cycle goes on.

A book that very much helped me during the pandemic and lockdown is *The Choice* by Edith Egar. It made me realise the exposed position or rather role I played in our blended family which in turn gave me the insight and the okay to address what I felt was creating a a quickly growing chasm between myself and my husband. It was my choice, which I took, to open up to him. We discussed, planned and acted together in partnership and came out the other side stronger.

I feel extremely lucky that I had an inner rage that encouraged me and kept me going during the end of my time with Brody. Often, I had thought… 'What could I do differently to get him to love me more?' however maybe it should have been.

'Why is he behaving in this way?'

'Why doesn't he want me to be me?'

An interesting observation or conclusion I have come to in recent years is that the healthiest of relationships is when you feel at ease to do anything comfortably regardless of whether the other person is there or not, because you are not being judged. Nor should you be.

Some readers may question that my experience was light in comparison to others they have heard. Yes, sadly, this is the case. Others have endured substantially more abusive relations than mine. Some readers will question why I had three children with Brody, which is justified. It was because I loved him. I wanted to be the one who fixed him, gave him the security he craved and provide the loyal family he never had and has never found since. Unfortunately, most people like Brody can't be helped, certainly not 'fixed' unless they seek professional help alongside loving family support. In the coaching and mentoring world, a phrase commonly referred to is:

'Words that move mountains.'

These words whatever they may be, spark action but only for those who are open to it. Sadly, many are not. Please don't be one of them. Stand up.